KT-223-457

AN INTRODUCTION TO
CHAUCER

COMPANION STUDIES

The General Prologue to the Canterbury Tales, ed. J. Winny
The Canon's Yeoman's Prologue and Tale, ed. M. Hussey
The Clerk's Prologue and Tale, ed. J. Winny
The Franklin's Prologue and Tale, ed. A. C. Spearing
The Knight's Tale, ed. A. C. Spearing
The Merchant's Prologue and Tale, ed. M. Hussey
The Nun's Priest's Prologue and Tale, ed. M. Hussey
The Pardoner's Prologue and Tale, ed. A. C. Spearing
The Wife of Bath's Prologue and Tale, ed. J. Winny
The Miller's Prologue and Tale, ed. J. Winny
Chaucer's World, compiled by M. Hussey

AN INTRODUCTION TO
CHAUCER

BY

MAURICE HUSSEY
A.C.SPEARING
JAMES WINNY

CAMBRIDGE
AT THE UNIVERSITY PRESS
1965

Published by the Syndics of the Cambridge University Press
Bentley House, 200 Euston Road, London NW1 2DB
American Branch: 32 East 57th Street, New York, N.Y.10022

© Cambridge University Press 1965

Library of Congress Catalogue Card Number: 65-19124

ISBNS:
0 521 05353 6 hard covers
0 521 09286 8 paperback

First published 1965
Reprinted with corrections 1968
Reprinted 1972

Printed in Great Britain
at the University Printing House, Cambridge
(Brooke Crutchley, University Printer)

CONTENTS

PREFACE

This book provides the student, the teacher and the interested general reader with a serviceable and not too bulky introduction to Chaucer. It is meant as a 'first book' which will give a general orientation; the student should then go on to the specialist literature which deals in greater detail with many points which are here only touched on.

The book was planned to accompany the series of texts edited by the authors of these chapters, and published by the Cambridge University Press under the general series title 'Selected Tales of Chaucer'. An advantage of this kind of volume, standing at the head of such a series, is that within the individual volumes of text it is not necessary to do more than allude to the topics covered here. The editorial matter in the series of texts can thus concentrate on the particular Tales being studied, while here certain general topics can be treated once, and at length. This book will also be useful, we hope, to readers using a different edition of the Tales.

The text of Chaucer used in this book is that of F. N. Robinson (*The Complete Works of Geoffrey Chaucer*, 2nd ed., Oxford, 1957), modified in accordance with the principles followed in 'Selected Tales of Chaucer'.

M. P. H.
A. C. S.
J. W.

Cambridge
January 1965

1. CHAUCER HIMSELF

Geoffrey Chaucer the poet, son of John Chaucer the wine-merchant, was born a few years before the middle of the fourteenth century. The exact date of his birth has not been discovered; but we know that by 1359 Chaucer was old enough to undertake military service in France. The likelihood that he was born about 1343 is confirmed by a legal deposition made in 1386, which affirms Chaucer then to be 'forty years old and more'. He married at least once, and may have been the father of two sons, one of them the 'little Lewis' for whom he wrote a treatise on the astrolabe. Philippa Roet, whom he married in his twenties, possibly in 1366, died about twenty years later in 1387. Chaucer drew his royal pension for the last time in June 1400, and according to the inscription on his tomb in Westminster Abbey he died on 25 October that same year.

This fragmentary outline of the poet's life represents virtually all that is known of him as a man. That so little remains is hardly surprising. The still greater poet who lived two centuries closer to our own times is just as dark to us. Some hints of Chaucer's private life have survived, not in consequence of any contemporary fame which his poetry may have brought him, but in the record of his career as courtier and civil servant which is documented in state accounts. The scraps of factual information which support the broken biographical outline relate to Chaucer's diplomatic activities, and to his work as a servant of the Crown. They shed no light on Chaucer's personal character or the course of his domestic life. The depth of his religious faith or the colour of his political sympathies, his feelings towards his wife and the mood of his final years, are all lost in the dark backward of six centuries. Even with the help of official records, it is impossible to present a coherent account of Chaucer's life without leaning heavily upon conjecture and balance of likelihood. The impression which emerges is indistinct and tenuous, becoming blurred as soon as we concentrate our scrutiny upon it. What finally appears is the wide disparity between the man and the description of himself offered by the poet.

The record of Chaucer's public career reveals that he led an active professional life which could seldom have allowed much leisure for writing. It may be for this reason that several of his poems, *The Canterbury Tales* among them, were left unfinished. Although the court society to which he belonged knew of his poetry, it is doubtful whether his contemporaries would have regarded Chaucer primarily as a poet. His portrait of the Squire, who could 'songes make and wel endite', reminds us that accomplishment in the arts was expected of a courtier no less than horsemanship and prowess in arms. The Man of Law, it is true, complains that Chaucer has written so much that no story remains untold, and perhaps in this ironic allusion to himself Chaucer acknowledges that he has become famous as a poet. But we should not suppose that his professional activities took second place to his writing, either in Chaucer's private life or in the eyes of his contemporaries. However incomplete, the biography sketched by the official records of Chaucer's appointments and commissions probably gives us a fair idea of the man as his contemporaries saw him.

Although these records ignore the personal details which would most interest us, they indicate how broad an experience of life Chaucer could draw upon when he embarked on his great culminating poem. He came from a prosperous middle-class background, and entered the court while still a boy. We learn first of his service—probably as page—in the household of Princess Elizabeth, a daughter-in-law of Edward III through her marriage to his son Prince Lionel. This early association with the royal circle was to continue throughout Chaucer's life, with only a short interruption between 1386 and 1389 when he seems to have retired to Kent. The first indications of his presence at court appear in records of gifts from Princess Elizabeth, first of clothing and then of 20s. 'for necessaries at Christmas'.

This was in 1357. A year later he may have been in attendance upon his mistress at the great Feast of St George, when Edward III entertained the King of France, captured at Poitiers and not yet ransomed, the King of Cyprus[1] and the Queen of Scotland, together with many other nobles. Towards the end of 1359, now seventeen or eighteen, Chaucer was with the English army in France, during Edward III's final attempt to enforce his claim to the French crown. Near Reims he was captured and held prisoner until March of the following year, when his ransom was paid. During the negotiations for peace, which were concluded in October 1360, Chaucer returned to France as an emissary, and carried letters between Calais and England. Subsequently, little is known of Chaucer's life for the next seven years. It seems likely that during this period he was taken into the service of the king, who had already shown his interest in Chaucer by contributing £16 towards his ransom money. When, in 1367, Edward III awarded him a pension of 20 marks[2] for life, Chaucer was described in the king's accounts as *dilectus vallectus noster*, meaning a well-beloved personal attendant. The term was conventionally used of courtiers in the king's service, but was not necessarily a form of words only. The gifts and pensions which Chaucer continued to receive throughout his life seem to bear witness to a considerable personal charm.

At the end of this obscure period of his life, Chaucer was about twenty-five, possibly married, and about to be entrusted with a series of diplomatic missions abroad. In the summer of 1368 he was issued with a passport and allowed £10 as travelling expenses for a journey whose destination and purpose were not recorded. From June to September of 1370 he was again out of England, as we know from letters of protection granting Chaucer immunity from arrest or lawsuit while he was engaged on the king's affairs during these months. What business took him abroad was not disclosed; but the purpose

[1] The connexion between Peter of Cyprus and Chaucer's Knight is noted in the commentary upon *The General Prologue*, l. 58.

[2] A mark was 13s. 4d.: thus the pension amounted to £13. 6s. 8d. a year. The equivalent in modern money might be forty times as much.

of his next visit to the continent, which lasted from December 1372 until the following May, was to take part in negotiations with the Genoese about the choice of an English port for their trade. It is a measure of Chaucer's diplomatic and business ability that he should have been entrusted with such a task before he was thirty, and evidence of the personal assurance which, whenever he depicts himself in his poems, he pretends not to possess.

This visit to Italy is generally acknowledged as a decisive experience for Chaucer. From Genoa he travelled south to Florence, a proud and beautiful city whose splendid architecture, painting and literature gave her an unrivalled reputation as a home of the arts. Even today Florence is able to astonish the northern visitor by the richness of her cultural treasures, and although Florence acquired much of her present beauty from the still greater artists of the Italian Renaissance, no medieval traveller could have entered the city without a sense of awed excitement. The effect of Chaucer's Italian journey upon his imaginative outlook is not to be reckoned simply through the influence of Dante, Petrarch or Boccaccio upon his own writing. Florence alone would have revealed potentialities of man's creative and artistic power which the much humbler achievements of fourteenth-century England could not have suggested. Contact with this dazzling new world may have given Chaucer's imagination the stimulus which caused it to break into vigorous activity.

Chaucer had given the first substantial proof of his poetic talent shortly before this journey to Italy. In the previous year the duke of Lancaster, brother of Prince Lionel and better known as John of Gaunt, lost his wife Blanche to whom he was deeply attached. What relationship existed between Lancaster and Chaucer before the duchess's death is a matter for conjecture. In serving first his brother Lionel and then his father Edward III, Chaucer could hardly have avoided acquaintance with Lancaster. Whether from affection or sense of courtly duty, Chaucer commemorated Lancaster's grief in *The Book of the Duchess*, one of the earliest of his poems known to us. The relationship between the two men evidently became very close during the years following. In 1372 Lancaster awarded the considerable pension of £10 to Philippa Chaucer for her services to his second wife, and two years later he granted Chaucer the same generous stipend. Much later in life Lancaster took as his third wife the widowed sister of Philippa, Katherine Swynford, who had borne him four illegitimate children. The link between the two families allows us to suppose that Chaucer was well acquainted with Lancaster's eldest son Henry Bolingbroke, who at the age of thirty-two deposed his cousin Richard and made himself the third of the English kings whom Chaucer was to serve.

Genealogical table showing the relationships of Chaucer's royal patrons

EDWARD III

EDWARD	LIONEL	JOHN
The Black Prince	Duke of Clarence	Duke of Lancaster
RICHARD II		HENRY IV

After his return from Italy in 1373, Chaucer was allowed three years of uninterrupted residence in England before being dispatched on a further mission abroad. The appointments and awards conferred upon him during this short period established him as a prosperous and influential member of society. In 1374 he was granted the tenancy of a house above Aldgate, in the city wall north of the Tower of London. Here Chaucer lived rent-free during the period of his married life. In the same year he was appointed Controller of Customs and Subsidy on all the wool, skins and hides passing through the port of London, with the condition that he should keep the records in his own hand: a demand, in effect, that he should not assign his duties to a deputy. As stipend, Chaucer received £10 a year, supplemented by an annual award of 10 marks in recognition of diligent service. Another valuable appointment came his way in 1375, when he was made guardian of two wards of court—legal minors whose estates he was authorized to administer. From this he gained a considerable further income. During the next year, Chaucer was awarded the substantial fine of over £70 levied upon an unlicensed exporter of wool. If his various duties kept Chaucer too busily engaged to allow much time for writing poetry, he had at least some material compensation. His total income over this short period has been reckoned as equivalent to several thousand pounds of modern money. More important than this, his work brought him into familiar contact with the characters and trades of common life—merchants, shipmen, civic officials—who were to mingle with the figures of courtly literature in his greatest poem.

At the end of these three years Chaucer was in his early thirties, and a citizen of wealth and consequence, with a responsible post and influential friends at court. His diplomatic gifts were now to be employed once more. Between 1376 and 1381 Chaucer's domestic life was again interrupted by several missions abroad. Of the first our only information is that in December 1376 he received a sum of money, probably to cover travelling expenses, in connexion with secret services on the king's behalf. Three months later Chaucer was in Flanders with Sir Thomas Percy, who had been seneschal of Poitou a few years earlier, again engaged on the king's private affairs. It seems likely that Edward III was treating for peace with the French after a recurrence of fighting. From Flanders, Chaucer is known to have travelled to Paris and Montreuil. He was again in France during two weeks of May or June of the same year, probably as one of the negotiators in a renewed discussion of peace terms, and was paid 40 marks for his services. These periods of absence abroad made it impossible for Chaucer to comply with the terms of his appointment as Controller of Customs. Accordingly, he was permitted to appoint a deputy to carry out the duties while Chaucer was engaged on state affairs.

In June 1377 Edward III died after a reign of fifty years, and was succeeded by his grandson Richard II, at this time a boy of ten. The change did not affect Chaucer's position at court. He was confirmed in office as Controller of Customs, the royal annuities granted to Philippa and himself were renewed, and his diplomatic activities continued. In 1378 he was abroad for five months, accompanying a mission led by Sir Edward de Berkeley to negotiate with Bernabò Visconti, lord of Milan, 'touching the expedition of the king's war' in France, which was still going badly. Chaucer's personal expenses seem to have been unexpectedly great, for although he received an allowance of 100 marks for the journey he overspent this sum by £20, for which he was not reimbursed until 1380. He was again sent to France in 1381. This time the business was a projected marriage between Richard II and a daughter of the king of France. Two previous missions with the same object had been dispatched soon after Richard's accession, both of which Chaucer may have accompanied. The project fell through, and in the year following the young king married Anne of Bohemia, a princess of his own age. There is a tradition that Chaucer's *The Legend of Good Women* was written at the queen's request, and that the poem contains a covert dedication to her.

After the mission to France in 1381, Chaucer's domestic life was undisturbed by foreign journeys for a period of six years. This period of settled residence in London, which brought him up to the age of forty-five, gave Chaucer opportunity to produce a succession of courtly poems crowned by *Troilus and Criseyde*. Beside this long and moving work, he found time to write *The Parliament of Fowls*, *The Legend of Good Women*, and the romance of Palamon and Arcite which was later adopted as *The Knight's Tale*; and to translate the *De Consolatione Philosophiae* of Boethius. His poetic development may have been encouraged during the later part of this productive period by a further increase of income which gave him still greater financial security, and by his release from the possibly irksome duties of the custom-house. The picture of Chaucer's daily life given by the Eagle in *The House of Fame* suggests how hard he may have been pushing himself. Kept busy all day, the Eagle asserts, when his 'rekeninges' were complete Chaucer went home to Aldgate, where

> In stede of rest and new thinges…
> Thou sittest at another book
> Till fully daswed is thy look.

We hear more about this dazed look from Harry Bailly, who mocks Chaucer as a timid, uncommunicative traveller lost in his day-dreaming. The obvious irony of Chaucer's references to himself warns us not to regard such remarks very seriously, but there is no reason to doubt the underlying truth of the Eagle's comment. Chaucer's poetry bears witness to his wide reading, both of literature and of scientific works, but the terms of his appointment as Controller did not allow him much personal freedom during the daytime. When, in 1382, he became Controller of the Petty Custom on wines and other merchandise, he was granted permission to appoint a deputy to discharge these new responsibilities. During the year following he was given leave of absence from his post as Controller of Customs for four months, and again for a month in 1384. Finally, in 1385 he was permitted to have a permanent deputy in this office too; so that now, although probably losing part of his stipend to his substitutes in office, Chaucer could devote himself to his poetry.

This period of leisure did not last long. A year later Chaucer's hitherto steady rise of fortune seems to have encountered a serious check. The king's personal extravagance and favouritism aroused growing resentment among commons and nobility alike, and in 1386 an opposition party headed by the duke of Gloucester and the earl of Arundel forced Richard to dismiss his chief ministers, and to accept supervision of his revenue and household. Although Chaucer cannot have been directly involved in this political struggle, he enjoyed the king's favour and could have been regarded as a member of the royal party. This might explain why, in the same year, he lost both controllerships and the house over Aldgate which he had occupied since 1374. But it is possible that he had already voluntarily decided to retire from professional life, and that he had been living in Kent for some time before he gave up the house over Aldgate. In 1385 he was appointed a justice of the peace for that county, and in the following year he was returned as member of Parliament for Kent. His withdrawal from the city about the time of the king's restraint by Gloucester's party may have no political significance. If Chaucer fell under suspicion as a man who had received marks of the king's favour, he may have found it convenient to reside outside England. In the summer of 1387 he was granted protection for twelve months during his absence at Calais, one of the few remaining English possessions in France. Apart from the fact that he was included in the retinue of Sir William Beauchamp, nothing is known of the circumstances which took Chaucer across the Channel.

Withdrawal from London and the immediate circle of court life did not bring Chaucer the happiness which he may have expected. Within a year or two his wife died, and in the summer of 1388 several writs were issued, authorizing his arrest on charges of debt. Possibly Chaucer was in low water for a time; but in 1389 the king asserted his right to administer his kingdom, and to have a voice in the appointment of his ministers. As a result of this bold move, Chaucer found himself preferred to the most distinguished of the various posts which he held during his career as civil servant, though also the most responsible and demanding. This was the office of Clerk of the King's Works, whose wide range of duties have been summarized by Professor Robinson:

He had charge of buildings and repairs in the Tower, Westminster Palace, and eight other royal residences, together with lodges, mews, parks, and other belongings. In 1390 he was given a special commission to attend to repairs in St George's Chapel, Windsor. It was part of his business, in the same year, to construct scaffolds for two tournaments at Smithfield; and, in addition to the regular duties of his office as Clerk, he was appointed in March to a commission...to look after the walls, bridges, sewers, and ditches along the Thames from Greenwich to Woolwich.[1]

Although the appointment may have rescued Chaucer from financial distress, in another respect perhaps it could not have been worse timed. Soon after giving up his posts at the custom-house, Chaucer had begun work on *The Canterbury Tales*. Some of the stories now drafted into this varied collection of tales had been written during the previous decade of Chaucer's life—the series of tragic anecdotes

---

[1] *Complete Works of Geoffrey Chaucer* (1957), p. xxiii.

unkindly attributed to the Monk, the life of St Cecile which became *The Second Nun's Tale*, and the romance of Palamon and Arcite. They had been written as individual works, unrelated by the great imaginative scheme that would enable Chaucer to bring together his company of sundry folk and their stories as a close-knit body of characters and tales. At some unrecorded moment after his retirement from London, probably in 1387 or soon afterwards, Chaucer saw how these unconnected stories could be brought within a unified design. His plan envisaged a work of panoramic diversity, held together by the fascinated interest in human character which forty-five years of widely extended experience had developed. It was one of those conceptions, in themselves apparently simple and self-evident, which seem to occur to men of great creative genius as they reach a climax of their power, with an accumulated knowledge of their craft and of human life ready to be poured into a comprehensive master-piece. *The General Prologue* outlines a scheme which demanded of Chaucer 120 tales, linked by passages of discussion and argument. Beside suggesting his confident vitality as poet, the project implied a belief that he would have leisure for such a vast undertaking. Chaucer can hardly have settled into his stride when the appointment as Clerk of the King's Works arrived, bringing him financial security at the cost of crippling his ambitious poetic design. Under such a flood of practical responsibilities, his work as poet must have been almost completely submerged.

There must still have remained some intervals of leisure. Moreover, the comparatively short tales which Chaucer had set himself to write could not have demanded such long periods of concentrated effort as the courtly poems may have required.[1] But apart from the weight of responsibility which Chaucer had now to bear, his new duties involved much travelling about the country, as well as planning and supervising work on the many buildings under his charge.

---

[1] The tales told by the Reeve, the Pardoner, the Nun's Priest and the Miller, written during this final phase of Chaucer's career as poet, run to 404, 506, 626 and 668 lines respectively. In contrast, *The Knight's Tale* amounts to 2250 lines.

It was in the course of such professional journeys that, in October 1390, Chaucer was attacked and robbed either twice or three times in a matter of four days. The shock of this experience, aggravated by the loss of money for which Chaucer was accountable, may help to explain his resignation from the post the following summer, after a tenure just short of two years. Possibly he was anxious to return to his pilgrims.

He was not to remain without an official appointment. Within a month of resigning this office, Chaucer was made deputy forester of the royal forest of North Petherton, in Somerset. The usual duties of a forester were to safeguard vert and venison—the deer and its natural cover—for the king's hunting, and to arrest poachers. Whether Chaucer undertook such duties, and whether the appointment obliged him to live in the west of England, we can only guess. If he had resigned a much more important office because its responsibilities had proved too burdensome, he would not willingly have accepted another appointment which promised merely to harrass him in a different fashion. The existence of *The Canterbury Tales* implies that Chaucer enjoyed sufficient personal freedom after 1387 to write most of the twenty-four stories which make up the collection. If the period from 1389 to 1391 is ruled out, as taken up by the demands of the clerkship, and if we accept Robinson's statement that none of the tales can be positively dated later than 1394, it must follow that Chaucer's duties as deputy forester were not very exacting. The fact that he was designated member of a board of Greenwich freeholders in 1394 suggests that he was continuing to reside near London despite his connexion with Somerset. Chaucer was still holding his appointment as deputy forester in 1399, when he took the lease of a house in the garden of Westminster Abbey. It seems fair to assume that he spent little if any time at North Petherton, and that there was now no substantial hindrance to his writing.

The closing years of his life were cheered by renewed marks of royal favour. In 1393 the king made him a gift of £10 in recognition of 'good service rendered' during the previous year, and a year later

Chaucer was granted an annuity of £20. In addition, he was paid £21 due to him as arrears from his clerkship. He must have earned the respect of Henry Bolingbroke, now earl of Derby, who gave him a scarlet robe trimmed with fur valued at £8. Supported by this friendship, Chaucer's private position was unaffected by the political crisis of 1399, which brought Bolingbroke to the throne as Henry IV. The new king confirmed the royal annuity granted by Richard II, together with the allowance of a yearly butt of wine, and conferred an additional stipend of 40 marks upon the poet. There was little time remaining for Chaucer to enjoy the affluence and respect which, if lost during the previous decade, he had now regained. Less than a year after leasing the house at Westminster he died and was buried in the adjoining abbey, the first of a long line of English poets to be honoured by burial within its walls.

We might assume that Chaucer continued writing up to the end of his life, and that the unfinished state of *The Canterbury Tales* is the consequence of his dying before the age of sixty. In fact, there are reasons for supposing that Chaucer abandoned his great work some time before he died. Although it must be difficult to tell at what date this occurred, the moral gravity of *The Parson's Tale* implies an absolute rejection of the comic spirit in which the pilgrimage had set out. This final tale is not an entertaining story but an entirely sober prose sermon on the deadly sins, delivered as an implicit rebuke to the levity which the pilgrims have shown towards the religious task they have undertaken. It involves a change of tone, and suggests a change of purpose, with which Chaucer is completely identified. The tale is followed by an envoy to the reader and a prayer in which the poet begs divine forgiveness for the 'translacions and enditinges of worldly vanitees' which have brought his soul into peril:

the book of Troilus; the book also of Fame; the book of the xxv. Ladies; the book of the Duchesse; the book of Seint Valentines day of the Parlement of Briddes; the tales of Caunterbury, thilke that sownen into sinne;[1] the book of the Leoun...and many a song and many a leccherous lay.

[1] 'those which tend towards indecency': meaning the fabliaux.

We cannot hope to discover what motivated this retraction, which includes some works, such as *The Book of the Duchess* and *The House of Fame*, against which no serious moral objection could be raised. Like the other poems, however, they celebrate love of a purely earthly kind; and Chaucer's encouragement to his readers at the end of the *Troilus* to reject the vanity of worldly affections

> And loveth him, the which that right for love
> Upon a crois, oure soules for to beye,
> First starf, and roos, and sit in hevene above

shows his awareness of the disparity between sacred and profane in literature. It seems evident that towards the end of his life these feelings deepened to the point where Chaucer felt obliged to repudiate all that he had written as a courtly poet, retaining only the 'bookes of legendes of seintes, and omelies, and moralitee, and devocioun' which comprise a minor part of his work. *The Parson's Tale*, probably written earlier, was brought in to strengthen this sobered purpose. Its narrator takes over the authority granted to Harry Bailly by superior right of moral leadership, recalling the pilgrims to the vital spiritual issues that have been overlooked in their delighted absorption in a game. His tale, which makes no attempt to meet the Host's condition of tempering instruction with 'moost solaas', leads directly into the retractions, and subsequently, as we may suppose, to the winding-up of Chaucer's great enterprise. Not even the drastically curtailed programme which required only one tale of each pilgrim had been completed; but both tone and substance of this final contribution show that Chaucer was no longer minded to play.

A summary of Chaucer's career as courtier, diplomat and civil servant reveals a man who led not a single existence but two distinct and seemingly incompatible lives. The varied professional activities which earned him marks of favour from three sovereigns, beside the satisfaction of worldly success, are in themselves proof of remarkable human quality. Chaucer evidently possessed powers of intelligence and discriminating judgement, and almost certainly a personal charm, which might have secured him a prominent place at court without any other recommendation. He must have been a linguist, speaking fluent French and Italian. The diplomatic missions which took him repeatedly to France, and at least twice to northern Italy, are likely to have demanded patience and resourcefulness as well as a realistic appreciation of political facts. As Controller of Customs, Chaucer could hardly have carried out his appointed duties without being familiar with the commercial and maritime life of fourteenth-century London, or without a businesslike ability to cope with a complexity of mercantile affairs. Later, as Clerk of the King's Works, the demands upon his physical energy, his practical knowledge and his powers of organizing a busy department may have been still greater. At the age of fifty, when he was working at *The Canterbury Tales*, Chaucer must have appeared to his contemporaries as a highly capable and widely experienced man of the world, no less at home in the custom-house than in the court; a seasoned traveller and negotiator, a reliable servant of the Crown, and a discerning judge of men.

These accomplishments, and Chaucer's successful career in the worlds of public affairs and secret diplomacy, amount in themselves to a life's work of some distinction. But in addition, Chaucer was a poet of such outstanding talent that his professional career interests us only as a foil to his still greater achievement as a writer. The task of reconciling these two aspects of the man, each demanding qualities at odds with the nature of the other, presents difficulties which Chaucer himself seems to have acknowledged. The experienced man of affairs contemplates the impractical dreamer who is his complementary self, and admits the incongruity by turning it to comic advantage. The Eagle in *The House of Fame* refers scornfully to the unadventurous existence to which Chaucer retires among his books, 'also domb as any stoon', after his day's reckonings, living as a hermit while other men interest themselves in the world about them. On the road to Canterbury, borne forward by a company of aggressively confident individuals, the poet struggles unsuccessfully to play his part in the entertainment, telling a childish tale which brings down the Host's fury upon his head as a purveyor of 'rym dogerel'. The practised judgement which Chaucer actually possessed seems to have sharpened his awareness of this other self, whose imaginative experience shared little common ground with the world of the diplomat and civil servant. From first to last Chaucer depicts himself as a hesitant and bemused spectator, making hopeful attempts to familiarize himself with an environment which he never properly understands. Only the growing mastery of his writing reveals the competent ability which Chaucer denies to his timid counterpart in the poems, and assigns to the characters whom he creates.

Because the poet and the professional man are dissociated so completely, it is useless to expect Chaucer's poetry to illuminate his biography. There is, for instance, little in his work to suggest his extensive acquaintance with the two most important countries of continental Europe. The references in *The Clerk's Tale* to the 'hilles hye That been the boundes of West Lumbardye', and to some of the cities of northern Italy, may derive from Chaucer's experience of the country; but the passage could have been written without personal knowledge. Similarly the stanza of *The Monk's Tale* which briefly describes the fall of Bernabò Visconti,

God of delit,[1] and scourge of Lumbardye,

reminds us that Chaucer took part in negotiations with this cruel tyrant in 1378, but without hinting at the poet's personal contact with the man. References so general cannot enlarge our knowledge of Chaucer's life. The earlier works, which deal with the dreamlike figures of poetic fantasy, illuminate neither his workaday existence nor his domestic affairs. While his professional self was superintending the business of the custom-house or negotiating with Genoese merchants, Chaucer's imagination was exploring the Garden of Love under the guidance of Africanus, or being carried by the Eagle through the upper air towards the House of Fame. The two *personae* have no opportunity of meeting, much less of combining as a single

[1] 'self-gratification'.

15

individuality. Only in *The Canterbury Tales* does Chaucer turn away from the idealized world of the courtly poems, and adopt as his subject the figures and activities of common life. After an ironically romantic opening, *The General Prologue* declares a commitment to solid material reality and the familiar objects of normal experience— leather boots and burnished metal, a bald head, sunburnt skin, a bristly wart. Chaucer's absorption in the world of fact might suggest that he is now writing directly of his actual experience, and that the Canterbury pilgrims are drawn from life. It seems to be established that some of these figures—the Host, the Shipman and the Man of Law among them—had a living counterpart known to Chaucer; but the character whom he forms upon this basis remains an imaginative creation, as before. In supposing that Chaucer had encountered the Monk or the Wife of Bath we discredit the poetic force which brings into existence the almost tangible beings who depend upon Chaucer for their vitality and individual character.

The only figure of the actual world which Chaucer's work represents with any certainty is that of the poet himself. The self-portrait offered in the poems is comically disparaging, but there is in the poetry a range and an intellectual confidence, supported by an ironic discernment of truth, which tell us much about the outlook and human character of its author. In *The General Prologue* Chaucer effaces himself as pilgrim almost completely, admitting his presence in the barest of phrases and venturing no account of his personal appearance or background. The poet has exchanged fantasy for un-compromisingly solid substance, but remains too much a stranger to the boldly challenging habits of this new environment to throw off his protective shyness. When it falls to him to tell a story, the Host has to drag him roughly out of his shell, mocking Chaucer's with-drawn manner with the scorn of a practical man of affairs towards a dreamer:

> 'What man artow?' quod he;
> 'Thou lookest as thou woldest finde an hare,
> For evere upon the ground I se thee stare.'

Then, softening his mockery, he encourages the pilgrims to treat their odd associate as indulgently as they can, and draws attention to the features which make Chaucer so comically unusual:

> 'Now war yow, sires, and lat this man have place!
> He in the waast is shape as wel as I;
> This were a popet in an arm t'enbrace
> For any womman, smal and fair of face.
> He semeth elvissh by his contenaunce,
> For unto no wight dooth he daliaunce.'[1]

The Host's admiration is obviously sarcastic, and Chaucer supplements the joke by disappointing the expectation of 'som deyntee thing' to follow, in a tale whose banality gives the Host ear-ache. Harry Bailly's disrespectful description of the poet may not misrepresent the facts. Chaucer had hinted at his corpulence some years earlier by making the Eagle rebuke his enjoyment of good living: 'thyn abstinence is lite'. The portrait of Chaucer drawn in the margin of the Ellesmere manuscript of *The Canterbury Tales* supports the Host's verbal picture of the poet. Chaucer is shown on horseback, with one hand raised as though telling a tale; a short, plump figure with an appreciable roundness above his belt. The face is mild and rather sad, its pensiveness accented by the wistful expression which the Host might have called 'elvissh'. Perhaps both he and the Ellesmere miniaturist attributed to Chaucer the conventional character of a poet; that of a dreamer, dazed by the visions of unearthly beauty or of moral truth which provide the subject-matter of so many medieval poems. If the Chaucer of real life seemed only half-aware of the world about him, this disarming simplicity of manner concealed an acuteness of perception which proves itself abundantly in the sly disclosures of *The General Prologue*. Harry Bailly's impression of the poet as a man lost in an enchanted maze of thought, and not lifting his eyes from the ground, misrepresents

---

[1] 'Make room, ladies and gentlemen, for this man, whose girth is as slender as my own. Any woman would be glad to have such a dainty little person in her arms, with his sensitive features. You might think from his behaviour that he was moonstruck, for he doesn't chat or joke with anyone.'

Chaucer absurdly. The man who set down the details of the pilgrims' costume and personal habits was not only a penetrating observer, but the one member of the company able to see the habits and outward appearance of the pilgrims as the index of inward character, even when their manners were designed to conceal this hidden self.

Chaucer's pretence of shy ignorance or incompetence is sustained throughout his work. With the major exception of *Troilus and Criseyde*, the poems are generally narrated in the first person by a detached spectator of the central events. In *The Parliament of Fowls*, as in *The Canterbury Tales*, the poet watches and reports from the fringe of the action, either overlooked by the participants or invisible to them. This passive function accentuates his role of naïve onlooker, observing without much critical understanding of what he sees. In the early *Book of the Duchess* the poet meets the grief-stricken Man in Black who represents Lancaster, and listens to the bereaved man's story of his wooing and happy married life without grasping the significance of his mourning costume and deep melancholy. Eventually the Man in Black has to explain the fact which the poet has been too impercipient to recognize for himself:

> 'Thow wost ful litel what thow menest;
> I have lost more than thow wenest—
> God wot, allas! right that was she!'[1]
> 'Allas, sir, how? what may that be?'
> 'She is ded!' 'Nay!' 'Yis, be my trouthe!'

Developed towards comedy, this dullness grows into the simple-minded innocence which allows Chaucer to concur with the Monk's scandalous opinions. It takes other forms. One of the characteristic activities of Chaucer's comic irony is to describe the behaviour of characters who grasp only part of the truth, while the poet appreciates all that is hidden from view. This device is used with poignant effect at the tragic climax of *Troilus and Criseyde*, when Troilus waits for his mistress to fulfil her promise by returning from the Greek

---

[1] 'You don't realize the true sense of what you're saying. My loss is greater than you can imagine. God knows she was all I have claimed her to be.'

camp after the exchange. Beside him on the wall watching the
approaches to Troy, his friend Pandarus reckons with the wavering
resolution which love hides from Troilus, and realizes already that
Criseyde will not keep her word. Troilus's idealistic faith does
not allow him to doubt her constancy; but Pandarus, knowing her
better, foresees the painful disillusion which Troilus is about to
suffer. For the lover, the slow dawning of realization will be a
tragic experience; but for Pandarus, realistically aware of the false
position which Troilus is shoring up with hope and assurance,
the approach of this personal disaster contains an element of the
absurd:

> But in his herte he thoughte, and softe lough,
> And to himself ful sobrelich he seyde,
> 'From haselwode, ther joly Robin pleyde,
> Shal come al that that thow abidest heere.
> Ye, fare wel al the snow of ferne yere!'[1]

The situation is typical of Chaucer in its contrasting depths of awareness. Troilus's limited knowledge is set within the greater circle of
Pandarus's comprehensive understanding, to be observed with the
same discernment as recognizes the human weakness of Criseyde.
Pandarus watches; the detached and knowing spectator of a play
whose main actor cannot foresee the tragic *dénouement* towards
which he is moving.

As general narrator of *The Canterbury Tales*, Chaucer takes up a
position similar to that of Pandarus, but which enables him to observe
and report from a double standpoint. His descriptions of the
pilgrims are at once naïvely uncritical and sharply perceptive. Himself the least distinguished of the travellers, he seems too much
dazzled by their exceptional qualities to notice the moral shortcomings which his commentary brings to light. So he remarks
respectfully of the Wife of Bath, 'She was a worthy womman al hir
live', adding by way of irrelevant afterthought,

> Housbondes at chirche dore she hadde five;

---

[1] 'What you're waiting for will come when the seas run dry. It's goodbye to
all the happy past.' The expression *haselwode* is sarcastic and incredulous.

as though the second remark proved the soundness of his judgement. A seemingly guileless comment is the means of disclosing the moral character which the Wife's social dignity does not quite obscure. Chaucer's simple, lively picture of the pilgrim acts as index to the moral being whom his random notes on dress and habits unobtrusively define. The technique is oddly indirect. Chaucer is describing figures devised by himself, not people whom he had met and seen through, and the weaknesses which he pretends to discover in the pilgrims are integral to his conception of their characters. Their misleading outward appearance is put up as a decoy, so that the reader must himself discover the pilgrims' inward reality, by looking beneath the gaudy individual habits noted down with such apparent lack of design. At the same time Chaucer is evidently satisfying a deeper purpose by pretending not to have noticed the tell-tale details which, in fact, provide the essential feature of his character-sketch. The critically discerning observer pretends not to be there, and to be represented only by the sharp-eyed but otherwise imperceptive, overawed pilgrim to whom Chaucer yields his identity.

Thus Chaucer's irony extends to himself, as an apologetic hanger-on whose performance falls woefully short of the high standard demanded by the Host. Chaucer can afford to treat himself disrespectfully. *The General Prologue* shows him writing with an abundant creative power, and directing a vigorous imaginative impulse with the confidence of complete technical mastery. It also reveals, with a subtle indirectness which enhances the effect of the disclosure, a judgement of human character as positive as the sheer literary accomplishment of the poem. Aware of his power, Chaucer could enjoy pretending to be incompetent and imperceptive. Ironically he credits Harry Bailly with the buoyant assurance which he withholds from himself as pilgrim; though the energy and critical discernment of *The General Prologue* suggest how much of Chaucer's own qualities has gone into the Host's character.

This pretence of being uncommunicative and withdrawn, and of allowing one of his own characters to take over the direction of the pilgrimage, might have been devised simply as a sophisticated joke. It is probably a good deal more than this. Chaucer stands in the same relationship to the Host as to the Eagle in *The House of Fame*, who carries him on a celestial lecture-tour which shows him the whole expanse of the universe. Like Harry Bailly, the Eagle is talkative and peremptory, overawing and subduing the helpless passenger whom he snatches up 'in a swap' and bears off

> in his clawes starke
> As lightly as I were a larke

—possibly another satirical dig at Chaucer's portliness. Unable to stir a finger, the poet is obliged to endure a long scientific discourse and then to make observations of the earth and the heavens under the Eagle's instructions, permitted to make only monosyllabic comments in reply. As in *The Canterbury Tales*, the poet is carried along by a genial but irresistible force who overwhelms him as much by his volubility as by the sheer energy of his being. In both poems he submits, letting himself be reproved and instructed by the vastly superior creature who has taken possession of him. Again in *The Parliament of Fowls* Chaucer is taken in charge by a guide who conducts him, with more vigour than politeness, to the blossoming dream-world where the birds have assembled for their yearly convocation. At the gates of the enchanted garden Chaucer hesitates, like a piece of metal trapped between the opposite poles of a magnet, but finds himself bundled unceremoniously forward:

> Ferde I, that niste whether me was bet
> To entre or leve, till Affrican, my gide,
> Me hente, and shof in at the gates wide.[1]

This rough handling gives the poet a foretaste of the disrespectful treatment which he will receive from Harry Bailly. Africanus refers to Chaucer's modest intellectual gifts in terms as direct and unflattering as the Host will employ, and although he recognizes a

[1] 'I was in such a state of alarm that I couldn't judge whether it would be better for me to go in or to turn back, until finally my guide Africanus seized me and shoved me through the open gates.'

possibility that Chaucer has some literary talent, the admission is grudging and sceptical:

> And if thow haddest conning for t'endite,
> I shal the shewe mater of to write.[1]

Still, his supernatural guide is ready to lead the poet through the garden to the great gathering of birds whose debate provides the main subject of the poem. Although, like the Eagle and the Host, Africanus seems scornful of Chaucer's limited gifts and personal timidity, he too proves himself an illuminating guide, whose energetic prompting impels Chaucer out of his prosaic existence into another dimension of experience. For the imaginative matter of his writing, the poet depends upon the help of this forceful, omniscient being whose vitality and confidence put his own awkward endeavours to shame.

The poet's reliance upon a supernatural guide is an understandably common feature of medieval poetry, which frequently centres upon a dream or vision. The poet finds himself transported into a mystifying country, and must find a tutor who will lead him through its curious landscape and explain the nature of the fantastic buildings or creatures which it contains. In the greatest of medieval poems, Dante is led round the circles of Hell and Purgatory by the shade of the epic poet whom he venerates as his master, and then left to explore Paradise by the guidance of his own reason, now purified and exalted. The religious allegory of *Piers Plowman*, and a great number of lesser medieval poems, link dreamer, vision and unearthly guide in the same fashion. In *The Canterbury Tales* Chaucer appears to break away from this literary convention by turning his back upon dreams and visions, setting the poet's adventure squarely in the world of everyday fact and surrounding himself by characters who embody the crude, vivid sensations of wide-awake reality. The functions of the supernatural guide are taken over by the Host, whose authority derives from his long familiarity with human impulse and behaviour in an environment as unmistakably actual as himself. His

---

[1] 'Just in case you have any poetic ability, I will show you a fitting subject to write about.'

standards are those of common-sense, and he feels little sympathy towards poetic fantasy, forcing Chaucer out of hiding into the rough-and-tumble of the story-telling competition and the plain terms of ridicule which greet his childish tale. Yet the poet remains an awed and apologetic intruder, as before; a bewildered observer thrown into the company of unaccountable beings whose talents and faculties completely overshadow him. He also remains the central narrator of the whole occurrence, relating all the events of the pilgrimage as his own private experience. To this extent *The Canterbury Tales* preserves the characteristics of the dream-poem.

Thus in his last work Chaucer continues to be influenced by the literary convention which he seemed to have discarded. It seems possible to explain why he retained this association with the form of the dream-poem. The supernatural guide may have no function beyond revealing—not least for the reader's mental comfort—the significance of the odd landmarks and creatures which puzzle the dreaming poet. But there are suggestive indications in both *The House of Fame* and *The Parliament of Fowls*, if not in *The Canterbury Tales* as well, that Chaucer was using the conventions of the dream-poem for a deeper purpose. The two shorter poems both describe a transcendental region which the poet visits under the tutelage of his supernatural guide, who acts as interpreter to its perplexing figures and activities. Brought into contact with the marvellous, the poet proves himself slow-witted, hesitant and unadventurous; strikingly unlike his guide, who, apart from his daring and quick intelligence, enjoys unrestricted liberty of movement. The great bird which snatches up Chaucer from the petty world where he sits poring over a book bears him effortlessly into the sky until the earth resembles an animated map beneath them:

> Now valeyes, now forestes,
> And now unnethes[1] grete bestes;
> Now riveres, now citees,
> Now tounes, and now grete trees,
> Now shippes seyllinge in the see.

[1] 'dimly'.

This soaring flight, and the unlimited vastness of physical space which is laid open to Chaucer, are emblematic of imaginative experience. As the Eagle takes possession of him, the poet's modest circle of vision enlarges rapidly until it includes the whole expanse of natural life, seen with brilliant clarity and a comprehensive, detached insight. At the same time Chaucer acquires from his tutor knowledge and understanding beyond the capacity of his ordinary self, and although dazed by his adventure he finds himself able to describe his wonderful surroundings in appropriately graphic language. When the dreamer is set down outside the House of Fame he reaches the exacting climax of his poetic task, which is to bring the House into existence through the force of his writing. To achieve this he must exert a creative power comparable to that of the supernatural architect of the building, working under the direction of the impulse which shapes its material into a unified structure of unearthly beauty. This impulse is the force of imagination, and the House which is the poet's destination is also his own imaginative work of art. To reach it, Chaucer depends upon the Eagle, who transports him from a humdrum environment to the sublime elevation where he can become the maker of the miraculous building which his poem describes.

The form of the poet's adventure suggests the deeper significance of the relationship between Chaucer and his guide. In his everyday identity the poet is the least remarkable member of society: a man without special gifts or professional expertise, who knows that except during the short periods of imaginative excitement he is a merely commonplace individual. These moments of imaginative possession transform him completely. He becomes invested with vastly extended powers of insight and knowledge, and a fluent creative ability enables him to give substance to his marvellous dreams. The fumbling figure of everyday life becomes submerged in the greater personality which takes control of him, and is driven forward with the assurance of intuitive knowledge which replaces the laboured, uncertain perception of his ordinary self. He now sees and grasps truth effortlessly, taking in a complex reality as though at a single glance; able now to draw upon all the resources of language to express himself, where at other times he is tongue-tied and incoherent. The wretched tale of *Sir Thopas*, which the Host cuts off disgustedly, represents the meagre abilities of the poet when his imaginative gift deserts him. When Chaucer admits the poverty of his repertoire,

> For oother tales certes kan I noon,
> But of a rym I lerned long agoon,

he makes a characteristic joke at his own expense which no reader will take seriously. But the comic figure who accompanies the Canterbury pilgrims is not Chaucer the poet, but the unremarkable being into whom the poet subsides when his powers of imaginative insight and expression fade. For the dispossessed poet to depict himself as naïve and uninspired is a joke with a serious side. Although the magnitude of his achievement proves the absurdity of Chaucer's imposture, the comic personality which he assumes throughout his work reflects an aspect of his actual character, as a poet who must become humanly commonplace whenever his creative talent dries up. So abundantly creative a writer as Chaucer might have been particularly conscious of the disparity between these alternative selves; one tirelessly inventive, the other earthbound and conformist. By mocking the imperceptive being who embodies his prosaic self, Chaucer expresses a relaxed confidence in his ability as poet. The undistinguished counterpart, who brings ridicule upon himself by attempting to entertain the pilgrims with a tale in rhyme, is one aspect of Chaucer's personality. His ironically amused treatment of this other self suggests how indulgently he regarded its potential challenge to his creative power.

Thus the poems offer no picture of the man Chaucer, and throw no light upon his domestic affairs or professional life. They relate not to the diplomat or customs officer but to the poet. They do not describe his journeys and conferences, but the imaginative experience which he recorded with critical detachment even while the force of creative impulse was whirling him about. He catalogues the oddities of the pilgrims dispassionately, from the standpoint of a spectator who must remain on the periphery of their circle. His detached commentary, and especially the covert disclosures which prove Chaucer's critical alertness, cannot be separated from the existence of the nine-and-twenty beings to whom he gives life. His creative act sets in motion the searching critical scrutiny which immediately judges what is being made. This imaginative reflex, simultaneously creative and critical, is one of the characteristics of great art.

The same critical awareness informs Chaucer's comic portrait of himself. Working at the height of his powers and producing the crowning achievement of his life's work, Chaucer never loses sight of the inconsequential being who is swept away and transformed by the rush of imaginative vigour which impels *The Canterbury Tales*. Chaucer stands outside his masterpiece, supplying its creative energy, and offering in place of himself an embarrassed puppet whom the Host treats with good-tempered disdain. Through Harry Bailly, who duplicates within the poem the critical function of Chaucer himself, he imposes order on the turbulent raw material of poetry which the pilgrims represent. *The General Prologue* and the later tales must of course draw upon Chaucer's acquaintance with contemporary life. His characters are not the merely fantastic beings who had peopled his early poems, yet nor are they such figures as Chaucer might have observed about him in London, or riding across Kent towards the shrine of St Thomas. The presence of the simple, perplexed dreamer who relates all that happens in *The Canterbury Tales* suggests that this poem too is the account of a private, visionary experience, set down by a poet carried away by the force of his feelings; though without losing the balanced judgement which his art demands. If the element of social realism in this culminating poem implies that Chaucer was now working directly from life, the bewilderment of the narrator and the irresistible personality of the Host offer contrary evidence. Chaucer has withdrawn from the fantasies of a poetic dream-world, but still admits himself overawed by the strangeness of his adventure, and by the dwarfing energy of the widely accomplished figure who takes charge of him. To the extent that *The Canterbury Tales* contains a self-portrait of its author, it reveals a poet whose identity is bound up with his writing, and whose experience impinges only indirectly upon the world of material fact. That there was another Chaucer is evident from the inclusive humanity and wide understanding of the Tales themselves, and confirmed by the official records of his professional life. About him the poet did not choose to write. Instead, he created a world of his own, placing at its centre the comic figure who is both parody and truth of the imaginative greatness which has survived as Chaucer.

2. CHAUCER'S ENGLAND

Though medieval England was largely an agrarian society and Chaucer was largely an urban writer, the second half of the fourteenth century will always be talked of as Chaucer's England. This is as it should be, for even if he is not the only writer of distinction in the period, he is the one who has provided us with the archetypes and folk-heroes of his day. If we travel in the oldest parts of England, we can imagine his people working in the villages and towns. If we imagine a group of happy young courtiers, they are the Squire and his friends; a group of pilgrims on horseback can only be going to Canterbury. It is said that the true folk-hero is the man who never really existed but whom we need to explain certain developments. Chaucer's characters fulfil this condition; we can even say of them, of Madam Eglentine for instance, that she is for us more vivid and real than any real prioress could ever be.

Because sociological analysis is what the poet himself seems to have been offering in *The General Prologue*, this poem, though not the Tales, is likely to be well interpreted by means of sociological insight. In this chapter we shall glance at a few of the data of medieval England, thus providing a little background for the poem. This may not help us read the text itself, but it will help us to deepen our contextual knowledge for it so that we are in a still better position to return and read the verse with understanding.

Basically Chaucer divided his society into the conventional three estates—the Knight (the nobility), the working man (the third estate) and the ecclesiastic (the Church). Yet at the same time we cannot fail to notice the aspirations, the upward movement, of people much more recently found on the scene for the first time. The Merchant, forcing his way into the pattern, is joined by the Wife of Bath, also a town dweller, an astute trader and a representative of a small but highly successful group of emancipated women of the day. As representatives of the professional people Chaucer also provides a physician and a lawyer, the latter an instrument of much change in land tenure. To round off the group of townsfolk there are the ambitious gildsmen, spurred on by the social pride of their wives. Social history can add much corroborative or explanatory detail to Chaucer's swiftly drawn figures.

This economy of detail might be due to lack of time. It seems highly probable that he lacked sympathy as well. He was aware of the social changes that these characters portend, but our impression of him is of a conservative writer. Although (or because) his father was a vintner, he seems to have associated the mercantile world with images of corruption. However, it is significant in this respect that John Chaucer was a member of one of the older-established trades and not of one of the newer ones whose money came from the developing cloth industry. As we shall see in the section upon merchant life in the capital, there was a battle for power between the old trades and the new, and the vintners sided with the victuallers who found themselves ousted by the representatives of the cloth gilds.

In the Middle Ages England was not an isolated island, but a European country with possessions on the mainland. Men travelled easily from country to country for visits, for education or for trade. Even in wartime, goods travelled across national borders and trade could be maintained. Chaucer's travels abroad were numerous and influential for him. When warfaring knights returned home from the battle and hung their trappings up in the hall to rust while they themselves took a renewed interest in their local manor courts or in sheer relaxation, merchants were up and down France and Italy on their own devices, seeing other countries as natural extensions of their trading areas and not as alien worlds.

The Constitution

During the fourteenth century England was constitutionally a most active country. Each town, city, borough and county sent its representative to Parliament to watch local and national interests; in Chaucer's day Parliament was slowly gaining power at the expense of the immediate royal council. At the present time in England the sources of power are still changing. Nowadays, the Cabinet is taking more and more decisions away from Parliament, while the House of Commons has much greater influence and control than the Lords, which formerly dominated. Though women now sit in Parliament, this was unthinkable even for a peeress in her own right in the Middle Ages. The bishops, who as lords spiritual once loomed so large in constitutional matters and were the regular advisers of the monarch upon secular matters, have dwindled in power today. In place of the modern member of Parliament for a county like Kent, the medieval parliament summoned a Knight of the Shire, and for one year, 1386, Chaucer himself was appointed (not elected) to that office. This gave him time, towards the end of his life, to reflect upon the government of his day. Any thoughts he may have had about the power of the people to resist their sovereigns would have been rendered more sharp and urgent in the very last year of his life, since by 1399 two monarchs in one century had been deposed and put to death. Not only was it possible to bring pressure upon the king by a threat to withdraw financial supplies, it also occurred for the first time in that century that a disastrously weak king could be deposed and murdered.

The Law

The process of English law has been a slow evolution, creating a system out of local decisions and cases. The task of codifying the law fell to the Lord Chancellor, one of the three main secretaries of the king. Parliament's task was to vote money and discuss revisions and additions to the law, while that of the local justices was to carry it out.

It seems that England was a law-abiding country by continental standards, yet it was probably expected, for instance, that a market trader would fail to observe all the rules concerning price and quality. It was natural that an offender paid a fine, went away and committed the same offence. Nor did the fines always increase for the second offence, so that the fine had the appearance of a tax which persisted until the law was revised. In any case, fines, like taxes, did not always reach the authorities, for they could be pocketed on the way by minor officials. Even so, the system worked tolerably.

From about 1200 the Chancery, together with the Exchequer and the Wardrobe, became separate and independent offices where once they had been part of the immediate household of the king. The Exchequer, which was responsible for the collection of taxes and the disbursement of the major items of royal expenditure, had originally met in an office under the king's close scrutiny and drew its name from the chequered cloth like a chess-board on which the money was added by means of counters. The Wardrobe, responsible for the household expenditure of the monarch, had originally met in a royal dressing room and kept charge of the king's seal for use on all royal warrants. Between these two departments there grew up a considerable rivalry and it was common for a monarch to turn first to one and then to the other for money for his war-campaigns, while the officials were inclined to create barriers and difficulties in his path. The controllers of these offices were often clerics since, as we shall see in the next chapter, the Church dominated education, first in the schools (especially those attached to cathedrals and monasteries) then in the universities. The Church was the source of capable and educated men, and therefore of State servants. If he did not concern himself too deeply with the effects upon the Church, the king could reward his administrators with bishoprics which supplied a salary at the expense of the Church and saved his own exchequer. Although anti-clerical feeling was expressed from time to time by politicians outside the Church, the inevitable change to a secular household staff for the monarch waited until the Reformation in the sixteenth century, when the administration of the State ceased to be the affair of the king's household, and was handed over to a 'civil service' more like that of today. The main effect was the secularization of the State, and a diminishing of the influence of the Church on national life.

Villages

The country which was subject to this rule consisted of about 10 per cent. townspeople and 90 per cent. village folk, who mostly lived in units of not more than 200 souls. It was true, as one historian remarked, that two London buses could carry away all the adult members of a small village. Most people lived in such villages, in small cottages of timber or a type of clay called clunch, with roofs of thatch, closely grouped and often collapsible so that they might be moved to a different site. Each village was more or less self-sufficient, providing its own priest, miller, blacksmith, carpenter, wheelwright and alewife. A few villagers, but not all, might require to go as far as the nearest market-town, and some had probably never left their native village for more than an hour or so; similarly, a few visitors, a pedlar or two and perhaps a friar, might come into the village. Left to their own devices, people made or bought within the village clothes and tools, assembled their ploughs and carts, needing very little more.

The fourteenth century was the period when village life was changing out of its feudal patterns. In certain parts of the country sheep-rearing was taking the place of arable farming and employing fewer men; the drift from the land into the cities was beginning. Once workers had bought their freedom, they could value themselves as citizens rather than villeins or serfs with an overlord. Under the older form of organization the lord of the manor could assess the amount of labour to be exacted from every worker on his estate, and this would constitute the villager's payment for the land he held by feudal tenure. A man might be required for one, two or three days a week, to do so much harrowing, ploughing, carting and so on, depending on the season of the year. Regulating and supervising this complicated system was in itself tedious and when it became possible to substitute a money-payment for labour-payment the routine was much simplified. For example, under the old system there were complications when the weather held up operations or when a holiday interfered with the week, since these could create a backlog of working days difficult to keep track of and exact.

The introduction of money-dues in commutation of labour-dues was simpler for the villein too, even if it was costly; while for the lord it provided money with which he could buy luxury goods from the towns. The lord himself felt freer to settle in a city, or go away on wars, when he could leave the operation of his estate to a bailiff or reeve or even lease his land freehold to a newcomer. The villein was at liberty to leave the land although he had fines to pay if he did so. When we investigate the money- and labour-charges that fell upon the agricultural worker at that time, we can appreciate his willingness to leave the countryside. If he withdrew his labour as a worker and as a potential archer in wartime he had to pay *chevage*. If he married one of his daughters to a man of another manor, and thus deprived the lord of future workers, he had to pay *merchet*. The lord's claim upon his best beast when he died was called *heriot*, while his lesser hold upon such things as the rights to cattle-grazing or wood-gathering on the lord's land was also subject to a scale of payments, as were the (enforced) use of the parish mill and, occasionally, communal oven. Once away from this system of dues and obediences, the freeman became a town-dweller working at a craft of his own choice; those who remained on the land acquired a greater sense of dignity when the services were commuted into a money-payment or rent.

Chaucer's awareness of the problems of village life was not as keen as his knowledge of the court or the town; but he glanced at the problem in its essentials in his characteristic way. We can take first of all his use of the Reeve, given power to administer the estates of a young absentee lord and able to derive a considerable personal profit from his cunning. He is hated as 'slender and colerik', associated with the 'deeth', and feared. That 'deeth' is probably the Black Death, which gave many reeves the freedom of loosened feudal ties and vacant tenancies. Statutorily, a reeve was nominated by the peasants as an intermediary between master and workers; in practice he could become an instrument of oppression. His appearance and manner give form to the common attitudes of the day towards his class; and Chaucer has made him one of his darker, more saturnine figures.

The Franklin, a free man, a freeholder and a man of inherited substance is another of the Canterbury Pilgrims who represents one of the changes in the social scene. His chance would come when a hereditary landowner decided to rent out his land to a tenant-farmer, and on Chaucer's showing such tenants could make a huge success of it. He is presented as a veritable horn of plenty, a Santa Claus figure, one who has clearly profited from his position in the countryside. Like his creator Chaucer, he is appointed a Knight of the Shire.

The Miller, as a comic figure, needs little attention here. One might perhaps point in passing to his hinted dishonesty. The Miller of the Reeve's tale is an out-and-out rogue. We turn instead to that figure of incorruptible industry, the Plowman. That he offers his services to others of his own free will suggests that he is a freeman no longer oppressed by the duties of labour-service to a master. His brother, the Parson, is shown at his side. They have both resisted the call to the towns where the one might have made more money in a trade and the other in a fashionable chantry. The parish priest is a symbol of the ideal place of the church in village life, the centre of stability in it, and the spiritual home of a man who exercises the pastoral task to which he has been called. These brothers, Parson and Plowman, are twin pillars of the village at its best. It was always the poet's way to embody problems in personalities: he instinctively chose the right symbols to express the strengths of feudal life conceived as an ideal. Yet the world Chaucer lived in was not that of complete idealism, it was a world created by social change, speeded up by the coming of the Black Death, and beginning the long period of transition to the present day.

The Black Death

The appearance of the bubonic plague in England in 1348, the outbreak known as the Black Death, accelerated all the social changes that had been slowly under way since the beginning of the century. To compute the extent of the mortality caused is impossible since it varied widely from place to place and scholars have failed to agree upon the figures. Perhaps between 30 and 50 per cent. of the population met their death from the plague, though in some places it was as many as 90 per cent. of the inhabitants. Even under this vast strain the social framework did not collapse entirely and the wars in France were not brought to a standstill. Suddenly, the remaining agricultural workers found their labour at a premium; if they chose to remain in the country they could secure not only their freedom but also a greatly enhanced wage for their services. Their demands were in some districts excessive; a royal directive of 18 June 1350 laid it down that the wage-rates of 1346 should be adhered to and that those who demanded or paid more were to be fined or imprisoned. In the towns similar demands were heard and wherever workers preferred to take to begging instead of working, the council took the unusual step of making it illegal to give charity to 'sturdy beggars'. Such controls were enacted again and again, a clear sign that they were an ineffective attempt to regulate a rapidly changing social pattern.

The towns

Exactly how to define a town in the Middle Ages is not always clear. While on the continent it may have been the case, as Henri Pirenne has said, that all towns were fortified, it was not so in England. Lying around many of them were suburbs and fields; the processes of village life were encountered in many places that are known as towns and cities. Pirenne also defines a town as 'living...on trade and industry and possessing rights, an administration and its own distinctive system of law which conferred upon it a privileged status'. Such an administration was liable to fall into the hands of groups of wealthy traders who had an eye to their own benefit and the rigorous exclusion of outsiders. Advancing their own status by wealthy and noble marriages the merchants pressed their advantages into the realm of trade monopoly and the pursuit of permanent oligarchic power.

Each town possessed a number of different types of gilds to unify the members of trades and industries. First in date and importance were the Gilds Merchant: these saw to it that no merchant could open a shop unless he were an accepted member of the gild. They laid it down that every shop should serve both wholesale and retail trade, each with its distinct period of time allocated to it. It was usual, quite contrary to modern practice, for the goods to be brought to the market by a manufacturer for merchants to buy. The producer worked to his own time schedule and set his own standards, simply hoping that he would make a sale. Since the merchant had not put in a prior order he was free to reject goods that did not suit him. It was also, to take the system further, the members of the Gilds Merchant who directed exports across the Channel and the Bay of Biscay, hiring the shipowner as if he were a modern taxi-driver. In this venture it was the merchant who stood to lose since he, like his primary manufacturer, had no advance orders to fill and simply hoped that he would find his market where he landed. In such a context we can more easily understand the title 'Merchant Venturer' that was given to one of their companies. Since merchants compensated themselves for their risks by making large profits, they were frequently under ecclesiastical criticism for the policy of buying cheap and selling dear. This seemed to the Church to be close to the practice of usury, or money-lending at high interest rates.

Humbler than the Gilds Merchant were the craft gilds. These developed in the thirteenth century, and concerned themselves with the organization of a single trade in the town, controlling standards of craftsmanship, conditions of work, punishment of offenders and entry into the trade by apprentices. In small towns allied trades combined to form gilds. Where it happened that the price-fixing practised by the gilds was judged to be against the public interest, the town authorities sought to regulate the regulators, dividing the town against itself. When this division continued it tended to prevent united action by the whole town, but that in its turn prevented serious conflict between towns, such as developed between different towns in medieval Italy. Much good work was done in the field of charity by all the gilds, which tended to look after members who were sick or poor.

Finally, we have the parish gilds which united members on a voluntary basis for social activities and charitable work. Banquets and pilgrimages were organized for the benefit of the members and funds were contributed towards the upkeep of town-walls and bridges, to the general advantage of the whole town. No matter what their trade was, members of such gilds all wore a common livery and became eligible for a place on the town council. From what we know of them these bodies appear to have been of value to the parish and did not encourage the overriding ambitions of members of some of the senior gilds.

London

In 1377 London had between 35,000 and 45,000 inhabitants, being three times as large as the next biggest English town, Bristol. Paris, with its 80,000 souls was far larger, while Milan, Venice, Florence, Naples and Ghent were all greater than London. Bristol, Norwich, York, Hull and Coventry were the other large English towns, but none of these had the advantages of the capital. Only Oxford and Cambridge, with their universities, possessed a more active intellectual life than London; but there were architects and artists waiting for commissions in the capital, writers and booksellers, as well as the nobles who constituted the king's court and tended to attract talented people to their own service. London's domestic architecture could not emulate the great Italian residences built at the same period and the whole city was too odorous for perfect comfort, pleasure or even hygiene. The Thames added the note of beauty and distinction that only a river can give, and without which buildings lack splendour and perspective. Not far away were the fields; the total impression was summed up in these words attributed to William Dunbar, the Scots poet:

> London, thou art of townes *A per se*,[1]
> Soveraign of cities, semeliest in sight,
> Of high renoun, riches, and royaltie;
> Of lordis, barons, and many goodly knyght;
> Of most delectable lusty ladies bright;
> Of famous prelatis in habitis clericall,
> Of merchauntis full of substaunce and myght:
> London, thou art the flour of Cities all.

Three kings who engaged in quarrels with the London corporations, John, Richard II and Charles I, suffered for their temerity. In Richard's time there was a state of virtual war between the gilds. Those connected with the food trades, such as the vintners, to which Chaucer's father belonged, had long been the dominant party on the aldermanic bench and controlled local legislation. Then during the thirteen-eighties it was as if a new political party had arisen to take their place: the cloth gilds, such as the drapers, took over. In order to account for their rise we have to look outside the capital to the West Country and East Anglia where sheep-rearing was proving a major factor in national prosperity.

Wool

Wool had always been a staple commodity, but the urge to increase the volume of trade came when it was realized that fewer labourers were needed to tend a flock of sheep than to tend the same fields in arable farming. Fewer wages needed to be paid, but more money could be made. One of the after-effects of the Black Death was that

---

[1] 'best of all'.

the land of dead tenants tended to be transferred to sheep farming. Where it had formerly been the custom to send raw wool to be worked in Flanders the whole course of the industry was deliberately altered as a result of State intervention, by taxation. In 1275 a tax of 33 per cent. was placed upon exports of raw wool, while only 2 per cent. was levied upon cloth in its finished state. At once the encouragement to export the finished product, and the need to prepare better cloth to meet foreign competition in the export market, forced the industry to alter its policy and its techniques. Flemish workers were encouraged to immigrate, and English workers to improve their skill. How the industry expanded will be seen from these figures:

	Exports	
	Raw wool (in sacks)	Cloths
1347	30,000	4,422
1392–5 (average)	19,000	43,000

Wherever the geographical conditions were right, with good grazing land, plentiful water supply and such essentials as fuller's earth, the industry expanded. The west of England, with its ports at Bristol, Dartmouth and Exeter, was one of the areas which prospered; it finds its literary record in *The General Prologue*. The Wife of Bath, a rich trader in her own right, proclaims her occupation by her fine home-made clothing, and represents the clothworkers of the western counties of England. When Chaucer notes that she surpassed 'hem of Ypres and of Gent' it is possible that he means alien residents in England at the time, rather than the workers at home in Flanders. Although Bristol was the largest outlet for the export trade of the area, there was also Dartmouth, further in the west, to serve it, the home of the Shipman with his barge 'the Maudelaine'.

Chaucer, in his office in the Customs House, was familiar with the organization of trade. He would have known that the Italians, with their superior book-keeping techniques, and their reputation as financiers and money-lenders (even to the English Crown), were the most active importers, while they left the exporting to those closer to the actual manufacture. Many Italians lived in London, sending others travelling abroad on their behalf, while they remained in their counting-houses, unlike Chaucer's Merchant who travelled abroad on his own behalf. For the purposes of business, western Europe was closely united; Chaucer himself had been abroad upon mercantile and diplomatic missions which familiarized him with the increasing tempo of national trade.

He turned a charitable eye on the Gildsmen who make up his pilgrim company. There was no reason why he should not. If they were a little overproud of their new livery and their smart knives, they were harmless enough. His ironical eye might light upon the fact that property was the only prerequisite for a position upon the town or parish council. The haberdasher and his friends are members of trades that remained neutral in the gild war in London. They all have socially aspiring wives in the background to motivate and perhaps to henpeck them; their Cook is their most unnecessary piece of exhibitionism; none of the superior pilgrims thought of such a precaution against the ill-offices of the innkeepers along the way. We know that ordinary craftsmen were forbidden to wear knives with precious ornamentation and these burgesses were openly flaunting them. As members of a parish gild they were comparatively powerless and therefore harmless; Chaucer's irony is mild.

In the case of the Merchant, Chaucer seems to have felt differently. Here is one symbol of the entire process of social change that we have been sketching in the last few paragraphs. His 'Flaundrisshe bever hat' is an indication of his connexion with the Flemish trade. It is his aim to maintain his financial reputation and credit by seeming prosperous even though he is secretly in debt. Credit transactions, usury and other dealings that make money beget money are essentially secretive activities. He knew how 'in eschaunge sheeldes [to] selle': in other words, once he had sold goods in Flanders from Orwell in East Anglia he had to return to England with what we should now call 'soft currency'. The rate of exchange favoured English money in the thirteen-eighties. Knowing how to manipulate the money-market he was therefore able to make a profit on the exchange; the way in which he did it is not revealed, but there is a hint of shadiness in the passage, and there were regulations against such transactions. London merchants of the time, such as Philpot, Maghfield, Walworth and Brembre, who were all concerned with the take-over on the London corporation, bore general resemblances to Chaucer's unnamed merchant. Chaucer's lack of sympathy may mean that he was apprehensive of the future in London and England as a whole when men such as he held the purse strings.

The magnates

Chaucer's concentration upon the middle reaches of society in *The Canterbury Tales* excludes those at both extremes of the social scale. More significant than his failure to mention the condition of the poorest labourers is his silence on the barons or magnates, who were almost as powerful as the king himself and far richer than the Knight. In the reign of Edward II, for instance, his cousin, Thomas of Lancaster, possessor of five earldoms and vast territories, carried on a long conflict with the king and refused to provide troops for his war in Scotland. The defeat of the English forces at Bannockburn was the more disastrous as a result. Those nobles who befriended Edward, notably the Despenser family, converted royal favour into territorial aggrandizement, while another group of barons led by the Mortimers led the final attack upon the king and overthrew him. The seriousness of these struggles for power and land can hardly be exaggerated, and they broke out again during the reign of the equally weak and unfortunate Richard II.

The Mortimer family is representative of the histories of others who emerged as powerful magnates in the fourteenth century. Roger Mortimer, who allied himself with Queen Isabella to overthrow Edward II, had inherited estates on both sides of the Welsh border, as well as others in England and Ireland. Having reached the position of Protector to Edward III he carried on the process whereby royal favour or supreme power solidified itself in extensions to family estates. For these earls there was no purpose in titles and power unless they were firmly based on land: to be eligible for an earldom the requisite income was high and once an earldom had been established it was necessary, by marriage contracts and purchasing, to hold enough land to provide for every member of the family when the earl at its head died. When Roger Mortimer was put to death by Edward III for regicide, the family, in fact, lost their estates. They slowly recovered over the next thirty years, little by little, until the position of the former regicide family rivalled that of the royal family itself. In 1373, Edmund Mortimer married a granddaughter of Edward III and gave rise to the final irony. His estates at that time stood third in size to those of the Black Prince and John of Gaunt and when both princes and Richard II had died, Roger Mortimer III was the next male heir to the throne, the candidate supported by the rebellious Percy family in the early years of the fifteenth century. King Henry IV, the son of John of Gaunt, who seized the crown, was the magnate who achieved the summit of political power, ousted the rightful monarch and established his own line on the English throne.

As a body, then, the magnates were obsessed with the enlargement of their estates, like rich men today, and avoiding huge death duties. The co-operation of the king was essential to the realization of this ambition, since it was feudal practice for a large portion of the estate to revert to the king whenever one of his feudal tenants-in-chief died. Edward III's conciliatory policy towards them allowed them to avoid this by putting their estates in trust so that younger sons and daughters could be provided for—and not the eldest alone—and the formidable retinue of retainers need not be dismissed. Here lay one essential difference between the old system of feudal tenure, which had no wages to pay, and the newer one in which contracts and payments were essential. To manage and control estates stretching over many counties the magnate needed a large staff of stewards, receivers, auditors and lawyers. If they worked exclusively for a noble they were said to be 'of his fees and robes' ('robes' meaning livery). They appeared on the list of retainers together with minstrels, heralds, and servants numbering hundreds, and they were attached to the lord not by holding land by feudal tenure, but by receiving fees.

The lawyers

At this point a new significance attaches itself to Chaucer's Sergeant of Law, who earned 'fees and robes' for his services and was retained by many for his skill in the increasingly crucial art of conveyancing. In the feudal age, with services counting for everything and money payments uncommon, there had been little need for what we now know as the solicitor's work of conveyancing. Yet it was at this time that we find a Lancashire knight accused of retaining men 'with his robes and fees' who were in reality 'malefactors who rode armed in company...against the peace of the lord king and to the great terror of the people'. And on the other hand, in a tract by Wiclif, we read: 'In men of law reigneth much guile, for they maintain falseness for winning and make lords to maintain wrongs to do wrong when lords hope to do right and please God and by their covetousness and falseness they purchase lands and rents enough and do many extortions'. The ease with which Chaucer's Sergeant worked his way through a mass of complicated restrictions to prove his client's entitlement to lands in perpetuity earned him his fees. Such acuteness was his own justification of his academic knowledge of the law and brought more profit than his position on the bench.

The combined financial strength of the English magnates made the income of the monarch look small. The Earl of Lancaster, in Edward II's time, had an income from his English lands alone of £12,000 a year and there were at least half-a-dozen others with £3000. A few of the greatest merchants possessed wealth that would be reckoned in millions of pounds in modern currency: William de la Pole once lent a sum of £100,000 while another merchant offered to equip a whole fleet. The political power that went with so much wealth was unlikely to diminish since the magnates established the precedent that their families retained the lands at death which would previously have escheated back to the Crown. Enlarging their estates all the time, collecting together great bands of paid retainers, some with the rank of knight, the magnates in the fourteenth century were themselves a factor in the decline of feudalism. Whereas, in Edward I's reign, the manorial system was still an active social force, the next decade after his death showed that it might not long survive.

Edward II (1307–27)

Edward II, who squandered a position of strength, is criticized by all writers with the possible exception of the dramatist Marlowe who is sympathetic towards him in his play. Edward was thought to occupy himself unworthily in acting, swimming and the practice of the arts, while his sexual abnormalities had the effect of endowing several young men with wealth, territory and position to the irritation of the established nobles who were excluded from his society. The defeat at Bannockburn set the seal of destruction upon him and the estrangement between Edward and his queen, Isabella, speeded the end. In Paris she met Roger Mortimer and conspired with him to invade England. Together they seized the throne and executed Edward. In so doing they showed how far powerful unscrupulous and disloyal subjects might go and gave the country notice that the richest families had no fear of weak kings.

Edward III (1327–77)

Edward III, the only successful monarch of his century, opened his fifty-year reign in 1327 under the protectorship of his mother and Roger Mortimer. After a three-year minority he conspired with the Montague family to seize Mortimer and immediately had him put to death. Most of the long reign that ensued was given over to fighting either in France, where there were extensive English possessions, or in Scotland, the northern ally of the French, and always ready to attempt an embarrassing raid when it might assist their cause. In 1333, 1335 and 1336 Edward won victories with which the memory of the fiasco at Bannockburn was appeased. The balladist, Laurence Minot, noted the effect in one of his songs:

> Skottes out of Berwick and of Abirdene,
> At the Bannok burn war ye to kene,
> There slogh ye many sakles,[1] als it was sene,
> And now has King Edward wroken[2] it, I wene.

Scottish campaigns, although revived in 1346, were little more than side-issues in the Hundred Years War which was fought to establish English supremacy over territory in France. In 1340 Edward claimed the title of king of France and leagued with the Flemish to defeat the French monarch. The English possessions at that time were grouped in Normandy, in the north of France, and in a much more extensive zone around Bordeaux and Gascony on the Bay of Biscay. English victories at Sluys (1340), Crecy (1346) and Calais (1347) all ensured Edward's popularity at home and guaranteed him a continuing grant of money for the wars from his parliaments.

It was mainly in the intervals between the campaigns that he felt the pressure building up from the magnates at home. While he was away they were under little constraint and the failure of the king to control them allowed for the permanent establishment of the large families who used the kingdom for their own purposes. As early as 1340 he had created friction with the bishops of Coventry and Chichester who were his councillors and encountered still more determined opposition from the Archbishop of Canterbury who threatened him with excommunication. The following year, the king relented and conceded the right of his council and Parliament to audit his finances in exchange for their compliance in the levying of taxation. For almost thirty years afterwards, there were amicable relations between them once Edward had been forced to accept the limitations imposed upon him.

---

[1] 'innocents'.   [2] 'avenged'.

In 1359 Edward sailed for France for the last time, bringing the war to an end in the following year. Not long afterwards the battle-front switched to Spain where his two eldest sons, the Black Prince and John of Gaunt, led armies to win back the Castilian crown for Pedro who had been exiled by his half-brother, Henry. The Black Prince, whose exertions caused the ill-health that killed him prematurely in 1376, won a decisive victory at Najera, and John of Gaunt, who became the greatest magnate in the country, married Pedro's daughter. In spite of Chaucer's apostrophe to this monarch as 'O noble, O worthy Pedro, glory of Spain', he defaulted on the payments to England and the episode ended without glory.

Richard II (1377–99)

In the thirteen-seventies Edward was ageing. None of the later battles had been as successful as the ones of the thirteen-forties. Queen Philippa died and her place was taken by the royal mistress, Alice Perrers, who consoled Edward till his end in 1377 and then decamped with his jewels. The crown descended to Richard, the son of the Black Prince, who was still only a boy. Since John of Gaunt had established himself as the most powerful member of the royal family in the latter years of Edward's reign, it was assumed that he would strengthen his own position as the senior uncle and protector of the young king. Gaunt, known to all readers of Shakespeare as the choric voice of English patriotism, was really quite unlike this image. He was exceptionally well connected by a series of marriages which added estates to his grasp. His first wife brought him the duchy of Lancaster, and his second the nominal title of king of Castile, though his third, originally his mistress and sister-in-law to Geoffrey Chaucer, was less well connected. He was the most militant royalist among his family and had the least patience with the common people. Shakespeare's use of him as the voice of impersonal patriotism is exposed as poetic licence when his real position is understood. He was not suffering the pains of a patriot when he saw

Richard leasing the 'farms and tenements' of the realm; he was fearing the sequestration of his own properties in order that the fruitless wars in Ireland could be carried on. The years of Richard's minority and reign were full of military defeats and the poet Langland likened the political situation to the fable of rats seeking to put a bell on the cat. Under a powerful cat the rats and mice were powerless:

> There ne was ratoun in alle the route for alle the rewme of Fraunce,
> That dorst have ybounden the belle aboute the cattis nekke.[1]

But at the accession of Richard a political mouse speaks up, and this signifies the general disorder of the court and the licence that the magnates assumed:

> There the catte is a kitoun the courte is full elyng.[2]

Gaunt's influence lasted until 1386, when he was replaced by his brother, Thomas of Gloucester, a more unpleasant man. Gaunt's interests had included the support of the arts and it was under his influence that Chaucer was advanced in social position. He had originally been a page-boy to the duke of Clarence but was no longer in his court at the time of writing his first long poem, *The Book of the Duchess*, which commemorates Gaunt's first wife, Blanche. Though the poet's fortunes are associated with Gaunt it does not appear that he had ever taken his robes or become a member of his vast army of retainers. The three-year protectorship of Gloucester put a stop to Chaucer's political career; this suggests that the poet was a member of Gaunt's court circle important enough to merit ostracism and silencing during Gaunt's own eclipse.

The Peasants' Revolt

The crisis of 1381 which first brought Richard II as a boy of fourteen on to the political stage was the result of all the powerful forces that had been reshaping the social framework of the fourteenth century.

---

[1] 'There was not a rat in the entire crowd that dared to tie the bell round the cat's neck'.   [2] 'disordered'.

The Black Death contributed by the depopulation that it caused; the wars in France by the financial difficulties they created; the sense of unrest felt in every shire at oppressive measures was expressed most bitterly in it. The landlords resisted as long as they could the demands of villeins for freedom, since only by not paying wages and accepting labour-services could they expect to balance their own economy; the labourers demanded as a national policy a charter of liberty in which they were to pay 4*d*. an acre rent for their own holdings, instead of all the old manorial dues. Although this sense of discontent was well known in Parliament at the beginning of the reign of Richard, it did not prevent the government from levying a general poll-tax in 1357 and 1380, where each person was equally assessed. A sum that was trifling to a landlord was a penalty to a labourer and the folly of enforcing it in the search for supplies to keep the armies in the field in France was soon fully visible.

In 1381 the peasants revolted, marching upon London from both Kent and Essex, under their leader Wat Tyler. Property was destroyed in the capital and the Archbishop of Canterbury was put to death. John of Gaunt saved himself from the same fate by a fortunate escape to Scotland; only the personal intervention of the young king saved the capital from further destruction. Their demands granted, the crowds dispersed, although their leader had been killed. With the subtlety of a seasoned diplomat such as his uncle John of Gaunt behind him, the king revoked his promises and the rising collapsed. Later in life the king is said to have been reckless in his expenditure upon charity, as upon everything else, and it has been alleged that he was ashamed of the image he had presented to his people as a tyrant so early in his reign. Yet the movement has its claims upon our sympathy because it was the first time in English history when the peasants saw the importance of their position in society. They had been taxed as citizens on an equal footing with all other classes but they had been given no form of parliamentary representation. Nobody was prepared to give them a say in the government of the country for 500 years, but the rising was a prophetic declaration of rights. It has been pointed out that the success of village men as archers using their own weapons on the fields of France showed them exactly how important they were to the safety of the country as a whole. Returning home to England they proclaimed their importance to the peaceful running of the country and had the blessing of dissident members of the clergy to encourage them. The priest John Ball showed them that social equality and freedom were gifts of God towards men and that the landlords were conspiring to prevent their realizing these religious aims. Though he did not have this militant strain in his personality, Chaucer's Parson, content with his country parish and fully involved in its life, may have been intended as a cleric with tendencies that would now seem socialist.

The effect of all such movements towards agricultural freedom was that in the fifteenth century more and more landlords were conferring liberty upon the peasants and relying more upon financial contracts. The whole idea of villeinage was in decline, and demesne lands were leased at the highest figure to knights or freeholders, as John of Gaunt ordered in a letter of instruction to one of his stewards, 'without sparing anyone'. When villeinage died, the idea of feudal society went with it and in the fourteenth century we witness the slow death of feudalism, with the background noise of Jack Straw and his men in revolt accompanying it to oblivion. Chaucer makes a brief reference to the revolt in *The Nun's Priest's Tale*, showing that he was aware that he lived in a time of social upheaval.

Confrontation and conflict in the city were not restricted to the Peasants' Revolt. In the same year, 1381, another struggle developed when a member of one of the craft gilds, John of Northampton, rather than any of the candidates from the merchant bodies, became Lord Mayor. This was an issue that involved many who were far above the rank of the disputants. The victualling gilds were supported in their demand for a monopoly in the food industries by the king, so that it followed that the drapers' and other clothiers' gilds attracted the patronage of the magnates. A monopoly in food might have increased the cost of living and the struggle continued indecisively for several years. John of Gaunt, as the leading royalist, was a supporter of the victuallers but when he left the country to fight once more in Spain, not only the victuallers but a large section of the country suffered. Suddenly, in 1386, Thomas of Gloucester seized the Protectorship and struck at all who had supported his brother Gaunt, executing several and exiling others.

The Duke of Gloucester

At first Richard remained neutral, passively watching the outcome of the wave of hatred that was running through the royal family. He had his own advisers, chief among them Sir Simon Burley and the Earl of Suffolk, and he was prepared to bide his time. Gloucester ordered the death of Burley who was the king's tutor and a close friend of Chaucer; not even the pleadings of Queen Anne were of any avail. The Merciless Parliament of 1388 was packed by Gloucester to authorize treason trials. It left a sense of strain and fear in the country that a magnate, even though he was a member of the royal family, should be able to underprop his own desire with so naked a show of force. In 1386 after Chaucer was made Knight of the Shire for Kent he attended 61 out of a possible 71 debates for which he drew over £240, quite a fortune, in expenses from his constituency. Chaucer's was a long session and the consequences were two years away, but even so the poet seems to have been disillusioned by his taste of Westminster. He had long been familiar with diplomacy and probably thought Parliament, as it then was, something of a fantasy or joke. At least from the satirical treatment of their routine and language in *The Parliament of Fowls* (1382) this interpretation would seem correct. In that poem, for instance, the opening address of Nature resembles the convening speech of the Lord Chancellor. No doubt the stupider birds convey the writer's attitude towards some of the members. Derek Brewer, the most recent editor of the poem, points out that a number of specialized words found in it might well owe their origin to a verbatim study of parliamentary language: 'statute', 'ordenaunce' and 'common profit' are examples. It may be that this is only a witty poem and not a satire, but Chaucer must have been aware in 1386 how far he had advanced in the world since he had written that piece and how, under Gaunt's leadership, he had been promoted from one office of the Crown to another.

For three years, though, Chaucer disappeared from his offices and his life is obscure. He may have been significant enough to have been hounded out of office once Gloucester's purge was under way. He may have resigned to devote himself to poetry. When he wrote about the past in his poem, *The Former Age*, it seems probable that he was looking back to the time before rivalries and factions made London dangerous to live in:

> Unforged was the hauberk and the plate;
> The lambish peple, void of all vice,
> Hadden no fantasye to debate,
> But ech of hem wolde other wel cherice,
> No pride, non envye, non avarice,
> No lord, no taylage by no tyrannye.

In this context 'lambish' means innocent and not stupid; 'to debate' means either bring matters to debate or to allow strife to develop. The reference to 'taylage' recalls the unwise taxes of the thirteen-eighties which created widespread unrest and revolt. The iron age of political reality discouraged the writer, who seems to have preferred the world of courtly love and romance without such revenges and disloyalty.

Richard's personal rule (1389–99)

Richard waited one more year after the Merciless Parliament to declare himself monarch and open ten years of personal rule. From being a bystander he turned into an absolute ruler justified by the divine sanction of kingship. His revenge upon his uncle was richly deserved, though Gloucester's death is a standing reproach to Richard, if it was he who instigated it. Wherever the king turned he expected men to genuflect before him; there were even unpleasant scenes when he lost his temper. The most startling of these was when he struck the Earl of Arundel to the ground for arriving late at the funeral of Queen Anne in Westminster Abbey. He allowed his extravagances and his personal favourites the fullest rein so that he accumulated debts and intense opposition all over the kingdom. His idea of capturing military glory was to turn his attention from France to Ireland, a decision that was suicidal. A complete disengagement from war would have been more tactful since he was so short of money. What Parliament could not grant he took from the magnates in the form of war loans. Readers of Shakespeare's *Richard II* will remember John of Gaunt's grief at Richard's 'farming the realm', borrowing money and giving back in return nothing but certificates to show the generosity of the loan.

He welcomed back John of Gaunt in 1389 and ennobled his son Henry. Yet in the last years of his reign he exiled Henry and seized Lancastrian properties. Henry Bolingbroke was typical of his class and there is no possible surprise in what happened: Henry returned from exile, seized back his lands, imprisoned the king and put him to death. It followed the logical pattern of the period: magnate confronts monarch and overthrows him. Once more Chaucer's reactions merit attention. He knew both Gaunt and the future Henry IV quite well and in his poem, *Lack of Steadfastness*, he addressed Richard directly, though the monarch encouraged no public advice or speculations upon his intentions. Many a medieval king would have been offered such advice as a matter of convention, but when we compare the following words with the conventional ideas of the balladist, Minot, or Chaucer's successor, Hoccleve, we see evidence of bitter experience:

> O prince, desire to be honourable,
> Cherish thy folk and hate extorcioun.
> Suffre nothing that may be reprevable

To thyn estate don in thy region.
Shew forth thy swerd of castigacioun,
Dred God, do law, love trouthe and worthinesse,
And wed thy folk agein to stedfastnesse.

There was, of course, no worthy successor for Chaucer when he died in 1400. The other arts also tended to wither away under Lancastrian rule. Buildings were not extended and many of the newer craftsmen showed themselves less proficient than their predecessors. Only in music, with the work of Dunstable, was the fifteenth century capable of surpassing the era of Richard II. The king may have been either a madman or a neurotic, as some modern historians allege; we feel convinced that he committed political suicide as soon as he had his own way with his kingdom. In the light of such inadequacy it is difficult to offer his encouragement of artistic projects as extenuation of his weakness. It is these, however, that have lasted. We can still point to the picture of Richard II that appears in the Wilton Diptych or the contemporary portrait of the monarch in Westminster Abbey, to many illuminated manuscripts that he himself commissioned, the sculptures in Westminster Hall and Winchester College and the additions to English cathedrals in the new Perpendicular style of building. Minor arts such as the making of armour and tapestry, embroidery and metalwork, were all practised with distinction in the final years of the fourteenth century and have been amply described and illustrated in John Harvey's cultural history of the period, *Gothic England*.

Conclusion

The circumstances of Richard's death brought the hereditary guilt upon the Lancastrians which Shakespeare analysed in great depth in his cycle of history plays. Chaucer, who lived through events that were only items in a chronicle for Shakespeare, wrote little about them. William Langland would have been more bitter in his irony, but Chaucer made a gesture of protest and then returned to his poetic world which was inhabited by courtly lovers, social climbers and rapacious villagers. His realism was directed towards the middle reaches of society, he remained uninvolved as an artist in the presence of political violence. What is a poet expected to do on such occasions? Deny its existence, ignore it or face it? Chaucer's answer was to stop diplomatically short after admitting its existence. In 1413 Henry V ordered the reburial of Richard II and the poet Thomas Hoccleve took up the topic once more. We look in vain for a Shakespearean appraisal:

> See eke how our kinges benignitee
>   And loving herte his virtu can biwreye;
> Our king Richard that was, yee may wel see,
>   Is nat fled from his remembrance aweye.
> My wit souffysith nat to peyse and weye
>   With what honour he broght us to this toun,
> And with his queene at Westministere in th'abbeye
>   Solempnely in Toumbe leid adoun.[1]

The only success that Hoccleve scored with that poem was financial: his annuity of £13. 6s. 8d. was renewed.

It is tempting to call the new forces in fourteenth-century society Machiavellian. Their pressures were too great for any writer to ignore. Reading Chaucer's poetry we can find in it evidences of what we take to be the break-up of feudalism, our external knowledge of history lending new edge to the writer's perception and wit. But on the whole Chaucer relegated new elements in the national life to the spaces between the lines, where they still remain legible. In the last analysis Chaucer was more at home with festivity than with portent. The Wife of Bath is more typically 'Chaucerian' than the Merchant and the difference between the tales they tell must bear this out. It was not Chaucer's concern to discuss London life of the thirteen-eighties and thirteen-nineties in any detail; nor is there more than a hint about the oppression of the villagers by the reeves to balance

---

[1] 'See how kingly powers reveal his bounty and loving kindness; our King Richard that was has not been lost to the spirit of memory in us. My ability does not enable me to weigh up and consider what honour he brought to this town now that he is laid to rest in the Abbey at Westminster'.

the comedy of Robin Miller and his thumb of gold. Such familiar and amusing scenes as the Miller provides in his Tale give what we most value in the shape of poetic document. For that, of course, is what we have been doing: reducing creative literature of the highest order to the level of evidence or documentation. Chaucer was not aiming at being a medieval form of camera or tape-recorder, presenting exactly what was there and nothing else. The artist in him was concerned with his comic vision of life and controlling a literary technique to moral ends. When we read his poems we ought not to be saying 'how closely the writer mirrored the social life of his day' and pointing to the catalogue of details which make us accept his art as realistic. What we should be saying, instead, is: 'what a fine society it was to have provided the writer with a tradition that enabled him to write poetry that is so finely felt and finely executed'. In the words of the critic Raymond Williams, literature is to be read 'as a highly aware and articulate record of individual experience within a culture'. This is precisely what Chaucer's poetry provides within the society of medieval England.

3. THE CHURCH

The English Church in the fourteenth century fully deserves special and detailed discussion if only because Chaucer gave it such thorough—if oblique—attention. All Christian people knew that the Church took men under its care from birth to death and enveloped every branch of living with its ritual; offering at the same time a large field of employment for the most intelligent section of the population. Chaucer's view of the Church emerges as the picture is studied. It demands a separate account because much of it will be especially unfamiliar to us as we turn to Chaucer for his verification of the ideas of his day.

As to the size of the Church we find no complete agreement between historians. Thus in the thirteenth century, according to one historian, there were about 40,000 ordained members of the church (male) out of a population of about three million. On the other hand, a historian of the fourteenth century assesses the number of ordained members of the Church altogether as one-fifth of the population. This would amount to as many as 600,000, a number difficult to accept immediately. The difference would stem from different ways of assessing the evidence. It might also reflect an increase in the fourteenth century, but such a rapid rate is difficult to account for. It is fairly certain that at the time of the Reformation the Church owned one-fifth of the country's land and employed about one-tenth of the labour force. This becomes more comprehensible when it is realized that within its ranks it comprised those who today would work in the civil service, in science, medicine, estate management, education and other professions, as well as the direct service of God in the churches, chapels, monasteries, abbeys, friaries, chantries, cathedrals and convents. It worked ultimately as a branch of the Church of Rome, though the modern term Roman Catholic had not been invented, and its overlords in England were the two metropolitan archbishops: the Archbishop of York in charge of the northern branch and the Archbishop of Canterbury of the southern. Between them they administered sixteen dioceses or bishoprics, which were in turn responsible for the Church as it was represented in every village and town.

Chaucer's church representatives were carefully chosen; they were those members that might most frequently be seen by the average citizen. The bishops were too exalted to be within that range; Chaucer concentrated upon functionaries that the lower- or middle-class person was liable to meet. His catalogue opens with the Prioress and the Monk, who were fairly high in the scale; continues with the Friar and the Nun's Priest or chaplain; turns next to the Parson and the Clerk, and ends with the Summoner and the Pardoner who are left at the tail of the list because they were in a literal sense the dregs, and brought disgrace to the Church by their malpractices. To these, from a fuller reading of *The Canterbury Tales* we may add the Archdeacon in *The Friar's Tale* and the Canons in *The Canon's Yeoman's Tale*. They are, taken altogether, the people about whom there was most popular chit-chat, of whom there was a popular image. Had the Prioress been less worldly she would have been excluded from the list, but since she is the unique Madame Eglentine she is out in the world, and demanding inclusion.

The Church that Chaucer knew was almost a microcosm of the whole of society; further, its purpose was to try to civilize mankind in a period of wars, famines and plagues, and teach him the way to heaven. The corruption and sickness of society made some clerics preach that the world was in every way contemptible, and that death was the only way to happiness. Chaucer caught this mood in lines from *The Knight's Tale* which might seem the only attitude for a sensitive cleric to adopt:

> This world nis but a thurghfare ful of wo,
> And we been pilgrimes, passinge to and fro.
> Deeth is an ende of every worldly soore.

The quotation at once gives a further meaning to the poem's whole pilgrimage: we are all part of it, whether we take part in a literal pilgrimage or not. Those that travel today to stand in St Peter's Square in Rome may hear themselves addressed by the pope (probably in their own language) as 'pilgrims' even though they may think of themselves only as tourists. The pope sees them still as eternal pilgrims and life as a whole in the metaphor of the pilgrim's journey. In Chaucer's time the accent often fell sharply upon the need to take pilgrimages out of society or out of life, and religious excesses could develop from this attitude. The flagellants drove across Europe whipping themselves and their viewers in an attempt to strip mankind of sin and scourge him for his deadly guilt. These men also preached that the great plagues were sent as a punishment for wickedness, reaching out to everybody. In the end it must have seemed that religion was to be associated only with death and that the sooner Death came for Everyman, the happier he would be. The only optimism of any value was a long-term one, based on the happiness of the after-life; that alone was consolation for the short-term pessimism felt by so many writers and clerics. It is impossible to equate Chaucer with this attitude: for him religion had much that would enhance the life of the body as well as the life of the soul, and though he had reasons of his own for expressing some pessimism about the state of the world and the state of the Church, he was not likely to allow this to discolour his comic vision of humanity or his good-natured acceptance of what might follow this life.

It may be hazarded that the very size and complexity of the English Church was its greatest disadvantage. Many thousands of pounds had been donated to it at one time or another and many thousands of acres of land. Even within the Church itself there were doubts of the advisability of so many possessions. In the early Church, it was pointed out, there had been no endowments. The contrary view stated, however, that its social work demanded endowments and that the totally unproductive duties of the clergy would inevitably be curtailed without them. The debate on the matter within the walls of the Church is to be noted because it shows us that criticism of the work of the Church was never confined to external reformers; it could almost be said that it was a tradition of the Church to inspect and criticize its own shortcomings quite as much as it was a natural province for the jester, the satirist, the gossiper in the ale-house and the poet.

For Chaucer the work of this immense body was reduced to a number of specific and familiar personifications—just the people everybody knew—but even in the creation of these stock figures he was working from a quite different set of assumptions about its nature from any that we ourselves readily hold of it. Modern people appreciate old architecture—we are what the modern poet Philip Larkin has called 'ruin-bibbers', specialists in the architecture and other externals. Medieval people were attached to what Larkin calls 'the holy end', but were also delighted to have rights in the nave themselves. It was possible for them to see the Church as a suitable place for the congregation to hold a banquet or a 'church ale', while outside in the churchyard it was allowed to hold a fairly orderly dance or play. Such expressions of humanity are rarely fostered by the Church outside the Latin countries at the present day, and, to be fair, it must be admitted that there were also severe criticisms of congregational behaviour in this respect. The treatise *Oculus Sacerdotis*, by William of Pagula, gives rulings for priests on this score. It warns them against sedition, clamour, the songs and dances that enlivened many a vigil, and the stone-throwing that the people occasionally indulged in. The modern historian, W. A. Pantin, in *The English Church in the Fourteenth Century* (the standard book to consult), adds: 'The medieval public, by some curious trick of tradition or psychology, seems to have been irresistibly drawn to use churches and churchyards for the most unsuitable purposes', leaving the rest unsaid. There was room, clearly, for intense local pride in the parish church and sense of participation in all its concerns. Nine thousand of them, roughly, were to be found in England and these were the buildings that acted as the natural nucleus in every centre of population.

But the building is not the organization. To assess the Church we must inspect the member of the congregation quite as much as the member of the clergy appointed to direct him. The organization was as fluid as the material at its disposal, as learned or ignorant as the people that made it up. It was also something more mystical in nature. The modern Catholic novelist, Morris West, has expressed it in his study *The Children of the Sun* in these words: 'We distinguish between the Church and its members: the Church which is the mystical body of Christ, the repository of truth, the fountain of grace; and the members of the Church, priestly and lay, who use the truth and grace well or ill.' For the rest of this chapter we shall be concentrating upon the priestly group and analysing it as a hierarchy.

The pope

At the head of this immense empire was the pope under whom all the cardinals and archbishops served. In the fourteenth century there occurred the Great Schism which presented the scandal of two popes, one at Rome and the other at Avignon, and the problem of divided allegiance. This was not a typical occurrence and did not persist, but it deserves mention in the present study because the English rallied round Rome out of their instinctive dislike of the French who, to their discredit, supported the schismatic anti-pope. Relations with Rome were much taken up with diplomatic exchanges where London attempted to influence the pope in his selection of bishops from a list of candidates acceptable to the king. This difference of opinion was long-lasting and concerned the appointment of foreign clerics to English appointments and the respective right of pope and king to nominate bishops for vacancies in the country. Rome also made more direct contact with each country which owed her allegiance by sending out friars and pardoners whose work was aimed at reducing the delays caused by cumbersome international administration and intransigent attitudes at the council-tables.

The bishops

The ordinary layman in England could hardly be lucky enough to see the Head of the Church, but once or twice in his life he might see his bishop. Not all the bishops were equally assiduous in the task of visiting their dioceses, being too preoccupied elsewhere. These were not necessarily devout men chosen for sanctity but rather men who were noted for their diplomacy and administrative gifts. There were three medieval English bishops canonized for the sanctity of their lives: St Edmund Rich of Canterbury, St Richard Wych of Chichester and St Thomas Cantelupe of Hereford. St Thomas of Canterbury and St Osmund of Salisbury, further back in time, were more Norman than English. In general, we find in the bishoprics the highest point of a career open to talent. Those who were intent upon careers in medicine, teaching, law or administration would have to go into the Church as there was no other opening. Young men could not be asked to become saints in order to qualify for all these professions; the exercise of some of them is in itself a piety and a reward. If there were many clerics who were far less literate than most of us would consider tolerable, so there were those who had no overt pretensions to piety. A sense of responsibility and self-restraint could pass in its stead, and from intelligent men with these qualities the bishops were sometimes made.

It is, then, easy to criticize medieval bishops. Early representatives have become famous for sailing into battle and smiting the heads of their opponents. In the fourteenth century this was no longer done, nor did they smite the heads of their priests as they had once done. But a few of them were presented to sees at an absurdly early age if they showed the qualities that made the civil-servant type of bishop, such as those who filled the Exchequer or the Wardrobe or men like the gifted William of Wykeham. These were liable to receive the greater benefices and the large dioceses, while the pastorally minded were given the smaller sees. The more thrusting ones in larger offices were prepared to delegate more and more of their pastoral responsibilities to suffragan bishops, while they themselves played the absentee. Occasionally it happened that the suffragans called in were foreigners, and rarely seen, so that the routine administration of a diocese was left to the archdeacon, the dean and the canons who made up the cathedral chapter, and who thus acquired unexpected power and stirred up some of the anti-episcopal feeling that was rife during the century.

Chaucer nowhere depicts a bishop, a dean or a cathedral canon. He gives us a prioress; he invokes an archdeacon (suggesting that for such men, Hell was the purse), and in a brief ironical mention he suggests the qualities of an abbot ('A manly man, to been an abbot able', said of the Monk). His main task was with the members of the Church to be discussed next, the people familiar to his audience. Potentially, he valued the parish priest most of all, and this might be taken to imply very little respect for a system with so many loopholes for worldliness as to promote publicists and administrative giants instead of men of true humility and sanctity.

These views of the Church in the Middle Ages convey a portrait of a section of society that was still growing rapidly, encountering, as it grew, a whole series of conflicts. There was the development of national rivalry and war, especially between England and France. But the papacy was a secular power which had to preserve diplomatic contacts as well as assert ecclesiastical overlordship in Europe. Conflicts of rivalry and the pursuit of power between heads of states were duplicated lower down the scale by the bishops and the abbots, the parish clergy and the friars, with much intricate jockeying for position. Since money was so frequently in question, the greed of many men was called into play. If the king awarded a bishopric to a political servant, then the Church would have to pay the stipend; if the pope could appoint a foreign person to an English diocese, then England would have to keep him. For this reason there appeared the insecure agreements between kings and popes which broke down under pressure and caused international diplomats a vast and unnecessary amount of work.

The regular clergy: the monks

A large monastery was the most formidable emplacement of church-men that England had to show. Within its jurisdiction there were monks traditionally active in praying and working, copying manu-scripts or labouring in the fields. Such was the age-old pattern of the monks' lives. It often happened, however, that monasteries were endowed with money and lands that put them into the category of large landowners and produced a revolution in their organization. Monks were then required to spend their time more and more out of doors and further and further away from the monastery. It became the practice to institute small satellite- or sister-houses, known as 'cells' and it became common for monks, known as 'outriders', to be given the task of visiting the outlying estates. Chaucer's Monk was such a man. In the cells conduct could be a good deal more lax than in the mother-house, declining from the ideals laid down by Benedict. Such monks forgot the injunction 'laborare est orare' and let the manual tasks fall to the lot of domestic servants who were being engaged for the first time.

Monastic funds were spent on more lavish living and gradually even the largest rent-roll could diminish under the strain. How far the monks forgot the rules of chastity and obedience as well as that of poverty cannot now be said with certainty. For every account of immorality and excess recorded and reprinted today, there were many more blameless lives that neither sought nor received the lime-light. It was a part of the monks' fortune that they made their monasteries into such desirable hostels that kings and nobles relied upon them for free entertainment. A remedy they adopted was to appropriate the annual income of a church in their area, ousting a parish priest and putting in a vicar to supplant him. They profited from this in that the tithes would then go to the abbot (even after paying the vicar an annual salary he might be the gainer). New enemies were also created in the process and the tide of anti-clerical feeling was certain to rise still further in the area. The last resource in cases like this was to exploit religious treasures, and to encourage pilgrims and visitors who could be charged for accommodation and pestered for donations. The very success of the movement had caused its decline.

Chaucer's Monk is a harbinger of this decline. He is best understood as a gentleman-farmer or a business administrator in monastic robes, allowing himself the liberty of soft, furry linings so that the hard cloth should not prove too rough. Monks faced with the problems of landowning had to become sheep-rearers, bailiffs, evictors of tenants, rack-renters and enclosers of the common land like all secular landowners. To understand them we must see them riding over estates as a matter of necessity, abandoning the simple ideal of morning worship, a round of manual work, an afternoon of intellectual activity, and an evening of worship after a frugal meal. That was one of the 'old things' that the newer members of the Church had to let pass. Chaucer criticizes his Monk for accepting the security of the monastic life without accepting all the duties. Yet as an outrider and keeper of a cell he could do little else. The poet's complex irony points out in two directions at once. It satirizes the Monk and the growth of monasteries which made such Monks not only possible but essential. Yet Chaucer also admires the vitality in the man, the fact that he was a 'manly man' and he began to find extenuating circumstances when he recorded the cavalier tone of the Monk who said:

> Let Austin have his swink to him reserved.

It is significant that the aristocratic sport of hunting, to which he was so addicted, was forbidden to all monks. He might only fish in preparation for the days of abstinence when meat was forbidden. It is therefore suitable that Chaucer uses a fishing-image to describe the Monk:

> Ne that a monk, whan he is recchelees,
> Is likned til a fissh that is waterlees,
> This is to seyn, a monk out of his cloistre.
> But thilke text heeld he nat worth an oystre;
> And I seyde his opinion was good.

Can we criticize one of the executives for the administration of a business? This was Chaucer's dilemma and the source of popular criticism of the monastic orders. The Church's reply was to institute austere orders like the Carthusians and Cistercians and intensify their quest for the moderation, dignity, stability and authority of earlier monasticism: the misfortune was that reformations came so late.

The friars

To judge from the literature of the day as the mouthpiece of popular attitudes, one can only state that the friars, who came to England first in 1221, were less popular than the monks. Yet, they too had been sent out from Rome in an attempt to reassert the Christ-like virtues of poverty, chastity and total obedience. In accordance with the desires of the founder and pattern St Francis of Assisi, the friar who followed the Franciscan rule must live from day to day without possessions, and his main work was to be done teaching, preaching and begging out in the world. Since at first the friars had no churches of their own they needed the hospitality of the local parish church in order to operate at all. Failing that, they might preach on village greens and similar public places. Wherever they did they were assured of a congregation, for preaching was their principal talent. In an age devoted to the pulpit, the friars were the masters of the art, far superior to the average parish priest whose comparative ignorance of theology often hampered him and forced him to reduce his sermons to brief comments lacking the oratory of a skilled preacher.

The friars became successful; they established about 200 houses in England in one century, and were able to build their own churches. Pope Boniface VIII also allowed them to have wider powers in parish churches; this seemed to the secular clergy an invasion of their own rights and deepened the differences between the two. Their true function is hinted at by Chaucer's Host in *The Clerk's Prologue*:

> But precheth nat, as freres doon in Lente,
> To make us for oure olde sinnes wepe.

They were performing a spiritual task better than most of their rivals, yet nowhere do we find appreciative comments on their work. The sly characterization of Hubert was Chaucer's way of rendering permanent and concrete the half-formed image that would have been in the mind of many a Christian influenced by the parish clergy. The same critical valuation of their work and criticism of their hypocrisy we find in a complaint from the Canterbury clergy cited by W. A. Pantin. In a few sentences it brings before us both the Monk and the Friar:

These religious, to whom the quest of beggary ought to provide a living, go about with loosened reins, flowing with delights, on noble palfreys of their own, with saddles and reins most exquisitely ornamented, beyond the manner of the greater prelates of England...they are astute and one-sided middlemen, corrupt and disguised under the veil of religion... loaded with goods, they stuff their ruddy cheeks and blow out their bellies; and when they are deservedly rebuked for fomenting sin in this manner, they daily prepare intolerable plots against the English church.

How far have we come from St Francis, the simple 'poor fool' who renounced the world unconditionally!

Chaucer was especially biased against the friars: the Franciscans, the Dominicans, the Carmelites and the Austin friars. There is a legend, which cannot be substantiated, that he himself had had a brush with friars which exacerbated his feelings. There is similarly a legend that he was himself tricked by an alchemist living in Windsor. In that case, *The Canon's Yeoman's Tale* would have been the end-product of his irritation. The alchemist in that tale is a 'canon', presumably an Austin canon and another of the hated friars. Certainly Chaucer's treatment of friars does no justice to their excellence in the pulpit, their value to the community as university lecturers or the subtlety of their minds. The friar created in *The Summoner's Tale* is every whit as evil:

> And so bifel that on a day this frere
> Hadde preched at a churche in his manere,
> And specially, aboven every thing,
> Excited he the peple in his preching,

> To trentals,[1] and to yeve, for Goddes sake,
> Wherwith men mighte hooly houses make,
> Ther as divine service is honoured.

Franciscan churches, notable for their stained glass windows, were the object of their begging, but it was a constant temptation of the mendicants (as they were all collectively called) to pocket as much as they could. Preying upon the fear of hell was one of their favourite devices for extorting money. The same friar in *The Summoner's Tale* is capable of rendering hellfire in words of startling immediacy:

> 'Delivereth out', quod he, 'anon the soules.'
> Ful hard it is with flesshhook or with oules[2]
> To been yclawed, or to brenne[3] or bake.

It will now be realized that the immoralities, dishonesties and whimsies of Hubert are all traditional, a kind of summary of the prejudices of the period repeated time and time again. It is exceptionally difficult, as a result, to believe now that the friars were a credit to the Church, no matter how gifted they were as preachers and lecturers, simply because their public image was a continual scandal that nothing in Chaucer's day was able to correct.

The ingratiating manner of friars as confessors won them penitents, and Chaucer mentions this in his presentation of his Friar. He adds that their lenience with sinners was inspired by financial hopes. If this improved the status of friars in some areas, it was scandalous and monstrous to the bishops who reported on it. The Bishop of Armagh told the pope in 1357 that friars were breaking down the whole foundation of moral control. He pointed out that in his diocese he was aware of about 2000 cases of criminal behaviour 'of whom scarcely forty in a year come to me or my penitentiaries [parish priests hearing confession]; and all such men receive the sacraments like other men, and are absolved or said to be absolved'. The friars alone were thought capable of such reckless tampering with the Canon Law. Indeed in this they deserve the title given to later members of the regular clergy: 'the fathers that took away the sins

---

[1] 'thirty masses for the dead'.   [2] 'iron spikes'.   [3] 'burn'.

of the world'. It might be a means of endearing their orders to penitents in fear of excommunication but it could hardly fail to be a scandalous discredit to the Church in one of its most intimate and prized efforts at humanizing medieval people and restraining them from the violence that was all too often practised and encouraged by the social and political affairs of the day.

The nuns

The position of women in the medieval Church differed essentially from that of men. Few women could be spared from domestic life and from childbearing to devote themselves to the religious life, and those who were free came from a social background where living was elegant and courtly. In this light, it was natural that the surroundings of the convent should assume the character of a rich home. The official tasks allocated to nuns included singing divine service and attending to the needs of the young, the sick and the poor. In addition, totally enclosed orders such as the Carmelite nuns were expected to pass their whole day in contemplation and prayer, making amends, as some monks did, for the sins of their more active contemporaries. Unfortunately, modern historians have been forced to the conclusion that religious houses were ladies' clubs pursuing various works of mercy in the manner approved by their families but making little pretension to a life imbued with religion. Records of episcopal visitations to the convents confirm this judgement. Though, for some, the life of withdrawal presented many attractions, nuns were frequently anxious to escape it and, in spite of directives to the contrary, to join in pilgrimages.

Chaucer's Madame Eglentine suits the world of the elegant country club in every respect. In this she was typical of the common pattern of nuns who ought normally to have remained unseen and in seclusion. Chaucer's irony reaches out in two directions yet again. He glances at the institution whose function was to shut so fine a woman from a full life and he glances at her failure to live up to the demands of the institution. In the fifty lines that he devotes to the Prioress, he has shown with gentle irony his estimation of the lady and his amusement in catching her aping of courtly manners, showing a good secular taste in clothes and jewellery and harbouring a love of pets rather than human beings of the less attractive sort. Very human she is, so much so that people have sought for the original. The attempt is misconceived. The origin of Madame Eglentine was the popular feeling of the period rather than the census of residents. It should also be more widely realized that Chaucer's translation of the *Romance of the Rose* contains two hypocritical characters (La Vieille and False-Seeming) who blossomed out in his later life as the Prioress and the Friar. The closing pages of that book give us a clear sense of the degree of realism of these two. What passes as realism is only an encrustation of detail in the verse which prompts us to the mistaken idea: 'it must have been genuine, it is so complete and perfect'. It is a device of medieval rhetoric which has deceived us; it brings us the moral valuation of the whole of a secular society upon its ecclesiastical arm.

Parsons

The picture that follows is for Chaucer, at least, far less ambiguous and pessimistic. Once free of the regular clergy, Chaucer's anticlericalism dissolves. The parish priest was possibly the only ecclesiastic ever met by those who lived in the remotest areas. To remain in this position in the public eye and not to attempt to escape was for many men the pledge of their genuine love of their vocation. Once all the royal patrons and papal nominees had been paid from the revenues, there was frequently all too little left for the churchmen at the bottom of the scale. The mightier magnates of the Church took most of the money, and the lowly members did most of the work. How poorly they were paid is impossible to say with accuracy, but sometimes they may have gained more than a skilled farmworker and less than a small farmer. If the priest were rector of a parish he was entitled to all the parish contributions, but if he were only a vicar placed in charge by a rector who might be another priest, a layman, or an institution such as an abbey, he might earn considerably less. Chaucer's Parson, who remains at his post and is not a hireling put in by another, is, of course, an idealized figure. When we read of the multiplicity of benefices held by certain people we wonder how many priests there could be in the country who were able to give their full attention to the members of a single parish. In the thirteenth century we read of a minister of the Crown with as many as 300 benefices and of another whose name appeared among the clergy of all but four English dioceses. While it became economically necessary for some priests to hold two neighbouring parishes as one, there was no defence of this abuse when the holding of a plurality not only made the rector a perpetual absentee but opened the small local flock to the mercenary and the wolves.

Once installed in a parish, there were three main religious duties that fell to the priest's lot, the inescapable functions that run throughout the whole story of medieval religion: he must say Mass, preach, and he must absolve sins. The second and third tasks were more important than administering matrimony or baptism and quite as important as saying Mass; for in these ways the priest could reach each parishioner in his own tongue and expect a clearer response. In order to help those who were not scholarly enough to compose useful sermons the bishops often issued instructions on appropriate topics and insisted that a distinct course should be treated in each church. In this way the people were to be made familiar with the claims of the spiritual order and the need to subordinate to it all their sensual desires. There were also directives issued for the guidance of those priests who were virtually illiterate. It will be recalled that Chaucer's Parson was a scholar, but he was an ideal. A scholarly cleric was more likely to be in a cathedral chapter or anywhere else than in a village church. It was possible to be ordained a priest and still have little idea of the meaning of the recurrent Latin of the Mass. Complaints about this are heard from bishops and archbishops throughout the Middle Ages. In the face of this disadvantage one can only underline the virtues of humility, sanctity and sensitivity. These may impress the congregation where the mental qualities of a scholar would be denied appreciation.

A document that brings home to us the intellectual needs of the medieval parish priest is a book entitled *Instructions for Parish Priests*, written by John Mirk, who wrote several works which bear upon the problems of an illiterate laity and a priest who is very little better educated. In his *Instructions* Mirk has a great deal to say about the administration of the sacrament of confession; he deals with other sacraments and investigates such issues as tithe-paying, the care of infants and children, and the wickedness of usury and witchcraft. He fulfils the elementary need simply to tell the priests what their duties were, in which one is startled to find such advice as the following:

> Tavernes also thow moste for-sake,
> And marchaundyse thou schalt not make,
> Wrastelinge and schotinge, and suche maner game,
> Thow mighte not use withowte blame.

Startled, of course, that priests should be ordained and still need such reminders as these, or the ban on such excesses as 'cutteded clothes and piked schone'. The familiar clerical portraits in *The General Prologue* all point towards the sin of pride in attire. Mirk takes his readers as he found them in life and offers them what they require. His work, *Manuale Sacerdotis*, brings us a debate between a good priest, 'the priest of God whose soul is in his hands always' and the worldly priest whose aims are 'to be well fed, well clothed, to lead an easy life'. Such books were offered at a late stage in a priest's development and as a substitute for a good seminary education which was not afforded in England until the sixteenth century. For lack of it the standards of the lower clergy were dismal indeed and their tasks unbelievably difficult.

Although there had been a period when marriage was permitted to the clergy, in the fourteenth century all in major orders (sub-deacon, deacon and priest) were obliged to remain celibate. It was not felt to be so necessary for those who had taken only the minor orders: doorkeeper, reader, exorcist and acolyte. To receive these orders, often simultaneously, fitted a man to be a parish clerk and to assist the priest in the celebration of the sacraments. To him we shall return in a moment. The state of enforced celibacy had one un-desirable result: many of the priests fathered illegitimate children. More than a century after Chaucer's death, the poet John Skelton, rector of Diss in Norfolk, held up his bastard son in the pulpit and demanded whether it was not as well formed as any honest madam's issue. One assumes an amused tolerance of such situations. Chaucer himself turned to the theme in *The Reeve's Tale*:

> The person[1] of the toun hir fader was,
> With hire he yaf ful many a panne of bras,
> For that Simkin sholde in his blood allye.[2]

The dowry was given to stifle criticism of the young lady's birth; Chaucer comments with familiar irony:

> For hooly chirches good moot been despended
> On holy chirches blood, that is descended.

In his character of the Parson Chaucer created a figure that de-serves the reader's fullest sympathy. He was one of the twin pillars of society, the other being the Plowman who laboriously tills the earth and helps his neighbour. Not all in the flock are so good. From the instruction books of the period we reach the conclusion that many labourers were unaware of the words of the main prayers, of the meaning of the commandments or even of the dictates of the moral law. The Parson, self-effacing, dutiful and altruistic, is a positive and unpretentious man, presented by the poet entirely without irony. He needed the tithes, the tax of one-tenth upon the produce of the faithful in the parish, but he was not prepared to submit defaulters to the extreme penalties if, perhaps through poverty, they were remiss. Expounding theology in the pulpit was in keeping with his intellectual cast of mind; his technique in the con-fessional was also equally praiseworthy:

[1] 'parson'.   [2] 'marry into his house'.

He was to sinful men nat despitous
Ne of his speche daungerous ne digne,
But in his teching discreet and benigne.

Everything he did was 'to drawen folk to hevene by fairnesse'. When
it is his turn to give a tale, it is an amalgam of the pulpit and the
confessional, a detailed sermon on sin, showing the social manifesta-
tions of each sin and advancing the necessary meditations and courses
to combat it. It draws the parson's task to its conclusion and gives a
kind of epitome of the work of the priests in some 9000 parishes:
'A bettre preest I trowe that nowher noon is.'

The clerks

Each parson needed a clerk to assist him, and some had the assistance of a curate; both of them were salaried. Either might well take
a school in the parish such as we find in *The Prioress's Tale*. The
best-known Chaucerian figure of this type is Absolon in *The Miller's
Tale* who took round the incense:

This Absolon, that jolif was and gay,
Gooth with a sencer[1] on the haliday
Sensinge the wives of the parisshe faste;
And many a lovely look on hem he caste.

Because he was an Oxford man, this clerk allowed himself a great
deal of sartorial elegance (directly contrary to Mirk's views on what
was proper for the parish priest) for Absolon had 'Poules windows
corven on his shoes'. The other young man in the same tale is full
of sensuality, low cunning, and inventive wit. Compare these two
with the Clerk in *The General Prologue* and it seems that the poet
intended us to juxtapose the three and form our own conclusions,
two inadequate examples throwing the other into high relief. And
yet we cannot forget that the Clerk of Oxenford is bleak and grey as
a figure, while his counterparts are warm and human, alive in every

---

[1] 'incense-burner'.

vein. Chaucer could never refuse to accept the manliness of man or womanliness of woman, or pass them by without a nod of recognition in which the moralist in him went momentarily disregarded.

Theological debate

We have mentioned Oxford, the source and school of English divinity in the later Middle Ages. Realizing how far its subtleties were from the majority of the clergy of the time, let alone the laity, it may be instructive if we ask what the trained minds of the period chose to discuss in religion. We may choose one or two themes that recurred in the debates of the period. One of the most important was the doctrine of Transubstantiation, which asserts that the bread and wine of the Christian Eucharist are truly changed into the body and blood of Christ. It is an action that remains totally invisible because it concerns not the external appearance (the accident) but the internal essence (the substance), yet though it is in no sense a physical change it is nevertheless a real one. Catholic doctrine on this topic has remained at variance with the thought of some Protestant churches, and it was in the Middle Ages that the basic discussions were held. Out of the declaration of this doctrine arose the Feast of Corpus Christi, the Body of Christ, and in order to celebrate it in many towns the mystery cycles of plays were held as a ritual entertainment.

The salvation of the unbaptized child was also much debated, and so was the question of belief in astrology, with the dependent question of predestination. On this score theologians presented the cases of Esau and Jacob, two men sharing the same heritage and the same stars who nevertheless developed very distinctly from their essentially different natures. The determinism of stars was here denied by the operation of freewill. There were debates upon the Immaculate Conception, the doctrine that the Virgin Mary was conceived without original sin because of the mission she was to play in the history of humanity as the Mother of God. The question of poverty and private property in the members of the regular clergy was discussed with considerable objectivity, as were the conflicting aims of theology as divine knowledge and philosophy as the summit of human study. Such subjects were reserved for the very few, and it was a slow process whereby the fruits of these deliberations found their way low enough in the scale to be recognized at all in pastoral work. Sometimes the discussions were centred in topics that affected the wealth and status of the Church, sometimes there might be a topic that was an exercise in pure logic. In his coolly ironic manner Chaucer turned some of the earnestness of all these debates into a game. He was not, as far as we know, a university man but he possessed all the subtlety of mind that one would hope to find in a medieval graduate. He needed no special university licence to ponder on the relation of Church and State, the two Swords as they were called, wielding the spiritual and temporal powers. In England there was a close working between the two, the fruit of endless compromises, but there were moments in which a statesman decried an ecclesiastic and the anticlerical feeling that had been repressed surged up all over again in an overflow that Chaucer could well understand.

Confronted with the notion of Transubstantiation Chaucer reduced the academic issue to a game played in a kitchen:

> Thise cookes, how they stampe and streyne and grinde,
> And turnen substaunce into accident
> To fulfille al thy likerous talente.

These remarks from the Pardoner involve the whole theory already sketched and handle the concept with an expertness suitable for this narrator but barely necessary for a popular tale. In an even more comic passage given to the Nun's Priest, he reduces the problems of predestination and dream-literature to the opinions commonly held in a hen-roost:

> But I kan nat bulte it to the bren
> As kan the hooly doctour Augustin,
> Or Boece, or the Bisshop Bradwardin,
> Wheither that Goddes worthy forwiting
> Streyneth me nedely for to doon a thing.[1]

[1] See a full note on this complex passage in the present author's edition of *The Nun's Priest's Prologue and Tale* (Cambridge, 1965).

So astute a poet, looking over the shoulders of the professional writers for theological tips, could take from them material he was subtle enough to use and relish. Though he had not the theological training of William Langland, his contemporary, who was in minor orders, Chaucer's dealings with the problems of university lecture-rooms are more widely intelligible and often better assimilated into the medium of verse.

The summoners

Two groups of people not found in the modern church remain; both virtually created for most of us by Chaucer: the Summoner and the Pardoner. The English Church accepted Canon Law as promulgated at Rome, having the power to add further laws of its own where necessary. In every diocese the role of chief magistrate in the church courts was played by the archdeacon whose word on the moral law was binding and went as far as the power of excommunication. In some areas his work was supplemented by rural deans; in all he would have the assistance of summoners (also called apparitors) who were, to all intents and purposes, police constables. Because the number of clergy in the country was so great, special courts in which they, together with laymen, could be tried for offences against canon law, were kept busy. It was part of the 'benefit of clergy' that clerics were not to be tried in the civil courts even for civil offences. For centuries educated men could claim their literacy as an exemption from certain punishments since, on the whole, ecclesiastical court penalties were lighter. The courts in the diocese were set up particularly to consider crimes which were magnified by the clerical status of the offender. To be convicted of immorality, witchcraft, perjury or heresy was a great deal more serious in an ecclesiastic than in a layman and it was over this area that the archdeacon was called to pronounce sentence.

A further word is necessary here about archdeacons, though they make hardly more than an indirect appearance in Chaucer. We all know of the 'erchedeknes curs' that the Summoner held as a threat over sinners. The same class of ecclesiastic is mentioned again in *The Friar's Tale* which returns to the attack on the summoners. The summoners were clearly hated, and nationally held to be corrupt and wicked in themselves as though the sin they dealt with had in some way rubbed off on to them. Archdeacons, however, were similarly accused, especially of being bribable. They have been defended on the score of their poverty and the exhausting complexities of their work which demanded a clear legal mind and a full command of a wide area of knowledge if they were to be of value. They were accused of starting legal proceedings in order to seek bribes, and even in sermons of the day, many of them fine sources for comment upon social topics, we find deans and archdeacons thus accused: 'Coveitous prelates of holy chirche...that setteth imposiciouns upon her sugettes and chargeth hem wrongfulliche in her visitaciouns, and maketh hem to pay hem that hem lust, or what they wole aske'. The preacher includes deans and archdeacons in the condemnation as officers of these prelates. When we read a list of the offences that passed through their hands we impute nothing but harm to the members of the Church. Chaucer's list of crimes in *The Friar's Tale*, for instance, is excellent ammunition for attacks on the Church:

> Of wicchecraft, and eek of bawderie,
> Of diffamacioun, and avowtrie,
> Of chirche reves, and of testamentz,
> Of contractes and lakke of sacramentz,
> Of usure and of simonie also.

In that list we have a nice confusion of official business and crimes, cast together with a skill that may remind us of Pope's *Rape of the Lock*:

> Puffs, Powders, Patches, Bibles, Billet-doux.

The archdeacon's task was to correct these errors and not to multiply them, yet the crime rather than the punishment has remained the dominant image.

Chaucer's Summoner, one of the most loathsome and dangerous

of all his characters, is an example of both personal and institutional corruption: the blame is quite equally spread. He receives bribes and will let a potential prisoner remain free to practise licentiousness if his palm is well oiled. In this he seems to have been typical of the day. Chaucer returns to this in *The Friar's Tale* where the summoner has new tricks to lead him to dozens of victims of blackmail:

> He koude spare of lecchours[1] oon or two
> To techen him to[2] foure and twenty mo.
> For thogh this Somonour wood[3] were as an hare,
> To telle his harlotrye I wol nat spare.

Nobody spared the summoners, who on Chaucer's showing were ill-educated, unable to understand legal procedure, and too corrupt to attempt to appreciate the moral distinctions needed to administer the system. The scholar John of Salisbury said of them, 'Their high office makes it their duty to keep God's Law, yet they keep it not'. Thus was the Canon Law faultily administered throughout the country.

The pardoners

A similar perversion of justice and order, upon which all later ages have agreed, is the activity of the medieval pardoner or quaestor, whose task was to sell indulgences from the papal court, to offer relics and to preach. Like the friars in this sermon-riddled age, pardoners were successful preachers and useful money-collectors. In the Catholic religion it is taught that after the forgiveness of sin there remains a certain residue of punishment to be expiated either in this world or in the after-life, in purgatory. It thus became the practice to pray for the release of the souls of the dead from the residual punishment and to perform certain rites in order to reduce it in advance. Prayers and fasting were both means of securing release from such punishment once absolution had been given, and it became the habit to devote money to sacred purposes for that end as well. Rich merchants endowed whole church foundations with this

---

[1] 'sinners'.   [2] 'inform him about'.   [3] 'mad'.

in mind. Pardoners, some of them laymen, but most of them priests, were sometimes guilty of misrepresenting their own powers in order to sell their relics and pardons. By 1390 Pope Boniface IX spoke out so forcefully that criticism of pardoners on their tours of Europe became the standard view of the rest of the Church. By initiating pardons and pardoners the Church had started something it could not control; giving power to such unscrupulous people rebounded with intense discredit upon the source of power itself.

The most notorious pardoner in our literature is presented as a stumbling-block to the faithful, an interloper placed in a parish church for a single visit perhaps, and able to undo the work of a parish priest by his solicitations. In every word of his famous Prologue and Tale Chaucer's Pardoner is alive. His hysteria comes to us in the loud hortatory tones and in the lack of a firm moral attitude towards the sins he is ostensibly condemning. His Tale shows two classes of man: the riotous and the dead. Here is summed up something which we sense in the late medieval psyche: on the one hand is the fear of death which leads some men to a life of riot; on the other is a rejection of the world which looks forward only to the future life. In spite of all his inadequacies the Pardoner still contrives to bring the people some form of spiritual enlightenment through the power that lies in the keeping of the Church. When he says these three lines we forget the pigs' bones and the confidence tricks:

> And Jhesu Crist, that is oure soules leche,[1]
> So graunte yow his pardoun to receive,
> For that is best; I wol yow nat deceive.

The man who admitted that he did not worry 'whan that they been beried'

> Though that hir soules goon a-blakeberied

can still work another to repentance as 'freres doon in Lente'. Here is the ambiguity that Chaucer characteristically loves to create. Beside this, John Heywood's interlude, *The Four PP*, which also presents a pardoner, is devoid of all subtlety, and in our own day the

---

[1] 'soul-doctor'.

Tetzel scenes in John Osborne's *Luther* are mere farce, 'strong scenes' for a particular actor.

Before we leave this unattractive pair, who cling together, we might ask whether their inclusion at the end of *The General Prologue* is not in itself a piece of subtlety. They were despicable as individuals, but institutionally they had the power of summoning and in many cases of absolving or pardoning lay folk. On a small scale they seem to act out the summoning of all mankind to judgement on the Last Day. This is what the Church was doing even when the individual members of the institution abandoned all interest in the spiritual obligations of their calling. Both men are shown to us as sick men, hysterical and a little mad, and this we should interpret in both the spiritual and physical senses. Had they been healthy they might have been included earlier in the list of ecclesiastics and their power as literary creations might have been diminished. Like many of Chaucer's creations they stem from the popular evaluation of living men and that is how they come to us: examples of her ministers that the Church had most cause to disown.

Pilgrimages

After dwelling on these two it is pleasant now to turn to the whole framework in which Chaucer presents them to us: popular pilgrimages. We are not really certain how they were all organized, whether or not there was a form of travel agency responsible for arranging the starting-points. We know more precisely why different people joined in. Some were there because of a promise made, under instruction, from their confessors; others were activated by voluntary motives. Perhaps a few would like to enjoy the scenery and the relaxation, prepared for the inconveniences that might attend upon the holiday. But for whatever motives they travelled it was a worth-while thing to join a company of pilgrims and seek out the tomb of St Thomas at Canterbury. While there they would join in a number of services, hear about the life and death of the saint, enjoy a number of more convivial occasions to balance the meditative calm of the rest of the stay and go back home with new ideas and the purpose of renewing their spiritual lives. In the imaginary pilgrimage that Chaucer created it is to be assumed that his pilgrims would reach the city by easy stages on Good Friday and stay there for the celebration of the High Mass of Easter Day before returning home.

But Canterbury was not the only place suitable for a pilgrimage. If people lived nearer Glastonbury or Walsingham, Durham or Salisbury at the four points of the English compass they could join groups riding to those shrines. Pilgrimages in those days proliferated like arts festivals today; in some instances it is difficult to imagine why the practice ever developed. Because Henry II ordered the death of Thomas of Lancaster as a trouble-maker in his realm, he unwittingly made his victim not only a martyr in the general sense of the word, but almost in the saintly sense as well. People flocked to pray by his dead body at Pontefract and gave unaccountable reverence to his felt hat. Mementos were sold and the apparatus of the modern tourist trade sprang up in embryo, to the annoyance of the king who tried to stamp it all out. Anybody restrained from taking part in the pilgrimage would have presented himself to the public as a martyr in almost the same way. Time had its revenge when Henry's descendant Edward II was put to death and, quite irrespective of the quality of his life, various people began pilgrimages to Gloucester in his honour. Simon de Montfort was another whose claims for canonization the Church took no steps to consider seriously, though there was evidence of considerable support. Pilgrimages had begun to get out of hand.

There were those inveterate and permanent pilgrims like the Wife of Bath who were not content until they had gone out of the country on a pilgrimage and could sport a collection of the tourist badges procurable at each centre. Shrines in every country were thronged. St James of Compostella was always popular for the palmer seeking strange strands; a visit to Rome or the Holy Land itself was the summit of a lifetime's journeying. The Wife of Bath speaks familiarly of 'thise pilgrimages' just as she refers to the moths and mites that find their way into her wardrobe. She relishes them for the merriment and for the sense of conviviality that could be derived from a company of new friends. The richer people were readier to unbend on a pilgrimage than on any other errand, since they believed, then if at no other time, in the universal brotherhood that the Church preached at all times. Storytelling and bagpiping might well have been the main sources of amusement; for those who lived on the roads traversed by the pilgrims they were sometimes sources of irritation. The pilgrimage was one of the most attractive emanations of the religious spirit in the Middle Ages.

Lollardry

The only sharp critics of pilgrimages were the followers of John Wiclif, known as the Lollards, who were reformers within the Church and held a number of Puritan ideas. Wiclif was an austere but intemperate Oxford philosopher, whose attacks upon the Church drew attention to its wealth and corruption and challenged its theologians upon Transubstantiation, Masses for the dead, and papal Indulgences such as the pardoners carried. His attacks were often loose and indiscriminate and his followers fell apart after having drawn attention to a number of criticisms that needed stating. The movement came to nothing because it lacked powerful support, even though it had the benevolent ear of John of Gaunt, its influential protector. The difference between Lollardry and many other voices of reform heard within the Church in earlier centuries was that it lacked a systematic basis and declined into an imprecise heresy, its most positive principle being its demand for a Bible in the vernacular.

For Chaucer the word Lollard was still a joke: 'I smelle a loller in the wind', says the Host, often the poet's *alter ego*. But the connotations of this word were to change. Although the Peasant's Revolt was in no sense inspired by Wiclif, and he himself died three years later, the movement seems to have taken strength from the activities of the rebellious peasants. Where they had been attacking 'the peccability of the pope and the fallibility of the fathers' they were preparing to take local action against ecclesiastical buildings and personnel. They created their own priests and organized the Lollard revolts in 1414 and 1431. The Friars were eager to stamp out their enemies, and for a time there was on the one side a fear that political sedition would ensue and on the other that in suppression an Inquisition would be set up.

Lollardry died out later in the 15th century, its place being taken by a number of orthodox thinkers who attempted to reform the Church more fully from within. St Thomas More and Cardinal Wolsey were two such reformers who were too late. Luther and Henry VIII had moved first.

Chaucer

An artist and public official like Chaucer was often brought face to face with the workings of the Church. Its architecture came into his province while he was Clerk of the Works during the building of St George's Chapel in Windsor as well as at Westminster and Canterbury itself. He may have been attracted towards the mystery plays of the period although there is distinct reference to them in only one of his Tales and that, paradoxically, in one of the bawdy ones, that of the Miller. The old carpenter in that Tale is a Noah-figure, building an ark and waiting for rain. The imaginary voice that Nicholas claims to have received from God the Father is a parody of the instructions given to Noah himself, while Alisoun is the troublesome Wife as seen in most of the popular dramatizations of Mrs Noah. It is in the same tale that Absolon is said to have played 'Herodes on a scaffold hye'. It is therefore possible that Chaucer had written the Tale with a performance of the mystery plays fresh in his mind, conveying a depth in the Tale with his parodistic addition.

The form that interested him most deeply is the sermon and its employment of theology. The Parson and the Pardoner each give sermons when called upon for tales, but the affinities of Chaucer's art with this extremely popular art do not stop there. In *The Merchant's Tale* there is a long mock-sermon on the desirability of marriage; the only aspect of it that distinguishes it as a burlesque and not as serious is the application and expense of so much valid reasoning to so unworthy a husband as January:

> And certeinly, as sooth as God is king,
> To take a wif it is a glorious thing,
> And namely whan a man is cold and hoor,
> Thanne is a wif the fruit of his tresor.

May, his young wife, turns to 'fruit' literally at the end of the story which ends in a manner devastatingly different from all January's naïve early assumptions. Still more impressive than this, though, is the manner in which the Wife of Bath handles biblical authorities and the words of the Fathers of the Church in support of her idiosyncratic views upon marriage. With a fine note of disingenuousness she asks:

> Where can ye seye, in any manere age
> That hye God defended[1] mariage
> By expres word?

The cut and thrust of theological debate were the lifeblood of Chaucer. Very few other writers would have seen a need for theological or biblical terms in any of these contexts, though there is no doubt that they would have been easily appreciated. The very act of going to one of the poet's own readings of his works was like going to a sermon: there he was at a lectern moralizing—what terminology could be more suitable?

The mystics

Curiously, it is possible for us now in some ways to go more deeply into the medieval English religious mind than contemporaries who probably had no means of knowing the texts of all the great mystical

---

[1] 'forbade'.

writings of the period. Richard Rolle, the first of these, turned away from Oxford to live a hermit's existence in Yorkshire and composed there a number of treatises and lyrics. Next we have Walter Hilton, author of *The Scale of Perfection*, the unknown who wrote *The Cloud of Unknowing* and Dame Juliana of Norwich, author of *Revelations of Divine Love*. There is a great number of shorter anonymous pieces, and the whole genre suggests that there were readers for the other such manuscripts that circulated, an audience accustomed to the language of religious contemplation. Most of their authors probably lived in solitary seclusion because the over-populated seclusion of the monasteries and nunneries was no place to contemplate God in: the existence of the many such treatises which have come to light is evidence of the strength of the Church in those days, since it presumes a public versed in the subtlest aspects of their faith.

The chantries

Another essentially solitary act of faith which has been criticized by Chaucer and many of his readers is the provision of chantries where mass-priests prayed for the souls of those killed in the wars and of the dead in general. In the portrait of the Parson Chaucer criticizes mercenaries and those who flee to St Paul's to seek a chantry for souls. But it might be retorted that the very provision of so many private religious foundations was a sign of the value ascribed to religion in that period. For gilds to keep chaplains, for nobles to staff chapels of their own and for colleges to insist upon the value of chaplains is not a sign of laxity. The Black Prince was known as the Protector of the Church just as his brother Gaunt was the patron of the Lollards and he gave immense wealth to it. Such work as that of the chantry priest can never show success in this life and to judge religion pragmatically is never sufficient or successful. The discredits of an ecclesiastical system speak out much more rapidly. Any historian is obliged to insist that the triumphs of a civilization include the churches it built, the religious art, drama and other literature that it encouraged and the theological and ethical tone that its language expressed. Chaucer's use of the devices and idiom of the pulpit suggests that religion had penetrated deeply into him, and that his verbal techniques flowed naturally from a nature that was imbued with its concepts.

Excommunication

Such a view of the civilization of the Middle Ages is not affected by the existence of hundreds of documents about naughty nuns and lecherous friars. The literary critic works from a poem or a play which changes through the centuries only to the extent of a word or two, or a few marks of punctuation at the suggestion of one editor and another. The historian operates differently: he creates history as he goes along by the process of selecting the documents he will use, in ignorance of those that might once have existed and are now no longer available to him. One writer, for instance can accept the idea of excommunicating the faithful as a sign of the weakness of the faith while another sees it as a strength. The Church was determined to draw people to heaven, but it was sometimes driven to abandon them as too obstinate and incorrigible to be carried along. Chaucer's Parson was 'ful looth... to cursen for his tithes' and to hand people over to the processes of Canon Law which involved the horrors of dealing (like the clergy) with the Summoner. Others were prepared to invoke the writ of excommunication which is written out in Merk's *Instructions*:

We accursen hem by the auchthorite of the Courte of Rome, within and withoute, sleping or waking, going and sitting, stonding and riding, lying above erthe and under erthe, speking and crying and drinking; in wode, in water, in felde, in towne; acorsen hem, fader, son and holy ghost.

That magnificent prose is disastrous in its implication. It was the final act and we know that those who heard the sentence could be stricken to the heart. A boatman, excommunicated by the authorities of the University of Cambridge, threw himself into the water, making no effort to swim: 'Alas that I was ever born, because I am damned by excommunication'.[1] The Church acted on these occasions out of a position of strength and not as a sign of petulance and weakness.

For all his many-faceted perceptiveness and wit, Chaucer cannot convey the whole of the Church's mission. Both Langland, his contemporary, and Dante, his predecessor, did it better. The Italian provides an unmatchable vision of the after-life, while the Englishman is preoccupied with Christ's task of redemption. Langland, like Chaucer, sees English people moving across the stage and in his vision the churchmen play an even larger part:

> Heremites on an heep with hoked staves
> Wenten to Walsyngham and here wenches after;
> Grete lobyes and longe that loth were to swynke,
> Clotheden hem in copis to ben knowen fram othere;
> And shopen hem heremites here ese to have.[2]

The same caustic gravity serves him when he turns from a satire on the hermits, untouched by Chaucer, to the more familiar friars:

> I fonde there freris, alle the foure ordres,
> Preched the peple for profit of hem-selven,
> Glosed[3] the gospel.

Langland had not the subtle allusiveness and diplomacy of Chaucer. He has nothing but the naked vision and the shuddering contempt. Heaven is there but Hell is there too:

> a dongeon there-inne,
> With depe dyches and derke and dredful of sight.

This is the vision that rarely strikes us from the pages of Chaucer, though it is essential that a writer should attempt to plumb its depths.

---

[1] The incident is quoted in full in Derek Brewer's excellent *Chaucer in his Time*.

[2] 'There were heaps of hermits with hooked staffs going to Walsingham, their women following behind. They were great clumsy louts too idle to work who had dressed up in copes to be distinguished from other men and made themselves into hermits to gain an easy life.'   [3] 'expounded'.

Chaucer was too human and too detached to do it. Langland strikes us as so committed that he may at times lack the emotional distance from his subject to find the satisfactory means of communication. In all the character-portrayals that Chaucer has left us there is a sense of scale. The Parson and his brother, the Plowman, are both totally good. The Clerk is good, too, but he has none of the fascination of 'hende Nicholas' in *The Miller's Tale*. The merely good lack a sense of vitality and vivacity and their Tales reflect it. It can hardly be an accident that most of the best Tales are told by the worst people: the Pardoner, perhaps the worst of all, has provided the Tale which is judged by many to be the best of all. Monk, Prioress and Friar are in between, and there can be nobody suited to the reading of Chaucer who does not know the co-present praise and blame that attach to the manliness of the Monk and the womanliness and courtliness of the Prioress. She has become a Prioress; he will become an Abbot in due time; and it is to Chaucer quite fitting that they should be, even though from another viewpoint the moralist in him does his duty and shows why such appointments are reprehensible.

Chaucer has been called a cynic, but this seems to be a false estimate, since it does not allow for the depth of his positive commitment to the Church and his long-term optimism. He is also in a stronger position because his judgements are so allusive, so fugitive, subtle and diplomatic: they refuse to state and be branded. His greatness is that he is witty withal, and human. He fails to reach the depths of the religious consciousness of his age and one does not ask that he should have probed it, since there were others ordained for that purpose. He criticized the Church as it has always been criticized, for when it is not we shall not be in this world. In spite of its contemporary critics, many of whom were within its own walls, it has never been stronger in the centuries that followed and rarely, except in the seventeenth century, have its adherents provided us with such subtle verse.

4. CHAUCER'S LANGUAGE

For most modern readers Chaucer is the supreme, and perhaps the only well-known, medieval English poet. But the period in which Chaucer wrote—the second half of the fourteenth century—is one of the outstandingly great periods in English literature, a period comparable, for its number of great writers, only with the ages of Shakespeare and of Wordsworth. The age of Chaucer is a time of extraordinarily varied literary achievement. Part of this variety is that of Chaucer's own work, ranging from lyric to *fabliau*, from dream-allegory to novel-like realism, from natural science to Christian philosophy. But at the same time as Chaucer was producing these works, there were also writing William Langland, author of *Piers Plowman*, a poem of urgent quest for spiritual truth, at once learned and popular; the anonymous author of *Sir Gawain and the Green Knight*, the greatest medieval English romance, a poem which uniquely combines fantasy and psychological realism; and Chaucer's friend John Gower, whose lucid and undecorated style is a perfect vehicle for narrative, and can grip the heart by what it leaves out as much as by what it says. Besides these poets one must also mention two great writers of religious prose—Walter Hilton and the anonymous author of *The Cloud of Unknowing*—and John Wyclif and his followers who first translated the whole Bible into English.

It can scarcely be by coincidence that this constellation of great writers appeared at the very time when the English language was completing its triumph over French as the language of business and literature in England. It is well known that as a result of the Norman conquest of England in the late eleventh century, the spoken language of the upper classes and the language of most imaginative writing became Norman–French. (History, science, and philosophy were largely written neither in French nor in English but in Latin, and it must be added that religious prose continued to be written in English, and so did some secular poetry—perhaps the best example is the accomplished mixture of beast fable and disputation in *The Owl and the Nightingale*, written about 1200.) An extensive French literature was composed in England in the earlier Middle Ages; but as the English kings lost their Norman dominions the situation began to change, and by the late thirteenth and early fourteenth century it was already felt necessary to preserve French in monasteries and universities artificially, by statute. In course of the fourteenth century this inevitable change was accelerated by the protracted Anglo-French wars and the partial break-up of the earlier intellectual and cultural solidarity of Europe. Statutes were now used not to preserve the use of French but to abolish it. In 1362, for example, Parliament ordered that French should cease to be the language used in the law courts. One vivid piece of evidence as to the resurgence of English in the fourteenth century is found in John of Trevisa's translation of Ranulph Higden's *Polychronicon*. This work was written by Higden in Latin early in the century, and in it he remarks that the English language has become corrupted for two reasons:

One is that, contrary to the custom of all other nations, schoolchildren here are compelled to give up their own language and to construe their lessons and their tasks in French; and this has been so since the Normans first came into England. The other is that the children of upper-class people are taught to speak French from the time they are rocked in their cradles and first learn to play with their childish toys; and provincial people insist on imitating the upper classes, and they take great trouble to try to speak French, so as to be held in higher esteem.

But when Trevisa came to translate Higden's work in the thirteen-eighties, he found it necessary to add a comment on this passage, pointing out that since the time of the Black Death (1349) this custom was changed. Nowadays, he says, 'in all the grammar schools in England, the children are abandoning French and are construing and learning in English', with the result that 'their left heels know as much French as they do'.[1] Thus grammar-school teaching began to be in English at the very time when Chaucer would have been a schoolboy.

The English that triumphed over French in the fourteenth century was, as a glance at any page of Chaucer will show, considerably different from modern English, and yet not so different that it cannot be largely understood by a modern reader. We must distinguish here between Chaucer's language and the other varieties of English that were used in the fourteenth century. Nowadays, although different dialects are still spoken in different parts of England, there exists a standard form of English, both for speaking and (still more) for writing. But in Chaucer's time there was no such national standard, and the different dialects were still used, naturally and unself-consciously, for literary purposes. Chaucer himself was aware of these different varieties of English. In the conclusion to *Troilus and Criseyde* he says to the 'litel bok' he has just written:

> And for ther is so gret diversite
> In Englissh and in writing of oure tonge,
> So prey I God that non miswrite the,
> Ne the mismetre for defaute of tonge.[2]

In *The Reeve's Tale*, Chaucer writes about two Cambridge students who came from 'Fer in the north, I kan nat telle where', and makes them speak an idiom which accurately represents that of fourteenth-century Northumberland or Durham and includes many words not used elsewhere in his work.[3] For him this northern dialect was a source of comedy: and Trevisa describes the speech of the 'Northumbres' as 'harsh, piercing, grating, and formless'. But it also seems likely that Chaucer knew of the alliterative poetry of the north, since he appears to imitate it in some battle-descriptions in *The Knight's Tale* and in the legend of Cleopatra in *The Legend of*

---

[1] These passages from Trevisa are most conveniently available in Kenneth Sisam, *Fourteenth Century Verse and Prose* (Oxford, 1921).

[2] 'nor scan you wrongly through not understanding the language'.

[3] See J. R. R. Tolkien, 'Chaucer as a Philologist', *Transactions of the Philological Society* (1934).

Good Women. Of the three great poets contemporary with Chaucer mentioned above, Langland wrote in a mixed south Midland dialect, the *Gawain*-poet in that of the north-west Midlands, and only Gower shared Chaucer's language, that of the king's court in London—essentially the east Midland dialect, but with certain southern elements. It is this medieval London English from which standard Modern English is descended, and this is the reason why modern English readers find Chaucer's language easy as compared with that of, say, *Sir Gawain and the Green Knight*. The latter is not intrinsically more difficult, but much of its vocabulary (including many Scandinavian words, since the north-west Midlands had earlier been under Danish rule) and some features of its grammar have not descended into Modern English. The comparative difficulty of the *Gawain*-poet's language and, incidentally, the brilliant use he makes of his unrhymed alliterative verse, may be illustrated by a brief quotation:

> And thenne he wayted hym aboute, and wylde hit hym thoght,
> And seye no syngne of resette bisydez nowhere,
> Bot hyghe bonkkez and brent upon bothe halve,
> And rughe knokled knarrez with knorned stonez;
> The skwez of the scowtes skayned hym thoght.
> Thenne he hoved, and wythhylde his hors at that tyde,
> And ofte chaunged his cher the chapel to seche:
> He sey non suche in no syde, and selly hym thoght.[1]

Chaucer's language is more accessible than this, but it does have certain differences from Modern English, and it may be helpful if some of these are explained.

The different dialects of medieval English are derived from the dialects spoken by the Anglo-Saxons before the Norman conquest, and these in turn come from the various but related languages spoken

---

[1] 'And then he looked round him, and it seemed wild to him, and he could see no sign of shelter anywhere round about—nothing but high steep hills on both sides, and rough rugged crags with gnarled stones; the crags seemed to graze the very clouds. Then he halted, and checked his horse for a moment, and turned this way and that to look for the chapel: he saw nothing like it in any direction, and that seemed strange to him.'   (Lines 2163–70.)

by the Germanic tribes who invaded England from the continent after the Romans withdrew. The processes of change from Old English (or Anglo-Saxon) to Middle English and from Middle to Modern English follow certain patterns, and can be explained by philologists in terms of regular sound-changes and the influence of one sound on another coming next to it. Here we shall be concerned not to explain the differences between Chaucer's English and our own along philological lines, but simply to note those differences that may cause a modern reader difficulty. But a single philological example may be given, to illustrate the factors at work. It will explain a common apparent irregularity in Chaucer's language. The Chaucerian word for 'day' is the same as our own; the normal plural ending in Chaucer's language is -*s* or -*es*; and thus we should expect Chaucer to write *dayes* for 'days'. So he does, sometimes; but he also uses the form *dawes*. The reason for this is as follows. The Old English word for 'day' is *dæg*, and it takes the plural ending -*as*. But the back vowel *a* in this ending influences the front vowel *æ* in the word itself, and changes it into another *a*. Now in Old English, *g* after a front vowel such as *æ* is pronounced as 'y', and so Old English *dæg* becomes Middle English *day*; but between two back vowels *g* is pronounced further back in the mouth to make a sound which in Middle English becomes *w*, and so *dagas* becomes *dawes*. The alternative plural form *dayes*, on the other hand, is formed simply by analogy with the singular *day*, and so we find the two plural forms side by side. Similarly in Chaucer, as the past participle of the verb 'to slay' (*sleen*), we find both *slayn* and *slawen*.

Grammar

We now turn to some of the main differences in grammar between Chaucerian and Modern English. We may begin by pointing out that in many cases, for various reasons, we find an -*e* ending in Chaucer which has been dropped in Modern English. This is unlikely to give any difficulty and will be mentioned no further.

Nouns

As in Modern English, there is only one normal inflectional ending: -*s* or -*es* in the plural and in the genitive. (It should be noted that the apostrophe found in the spelling of the genitive in Modern English was not used by Chaucer.) Also, as in Modern English, some nouns are unchanged in the plural (*sheep*), while others change their vowel (*foot*, *feet*) or add -*en* (*ox*, *oxen*). All these classes were larger in Chaucer's language than they are today. Unchanged plurals include words such as *yeer* ('Of twenty yeer of age he was, I gesse', *General Prologue*, 82) and nouns ending in -*s* in the singular (e.g. *caas*: 'In termes hadde he caas and doomes alle', *General Prologue*, 325). Plurals in -*en* include *eyen*, 'eyes' ('If that your eyen kan nat seen aright', *Canon's Yeoman's Tale*, 865) and *hosen*, 'stockings' ('Hir hosen weren of fyn scarlet reed', *General Prologue*, 458). Some nouns take no ending in the genitive singular (e.g. 'In hope to stonden in his *lady* grace', *General Prologue*, 88); these include all the nouns of relationship ending in -*er* (*fader*, *brother*, etc.: 'Now, by my fader soule that is deed', *General Prologue*, 783).

Adjectives

There are a few unusual forms which preserve the Old English inflections in the genitive. Thus in the singular Chaucer writes *alleskinnes*, 'of every kind', and in the plural he writes *alderbeste*, 'best of all', and *oure aller*, 'of all of us' ('Shal have a soper at oure aller cost', *General Prologue*, 801).

Adverbs

Some adverbs end in -*ly*, as in Modern English, others in -*liche* ('And have a mantel roialliche ybore', *General Prologue*, 380) and others simply in -*e* ('Ful loude he soong "Com hider, love, to me!"', *General Prologue*, 674).

Relative adverbs are often followed by *that* ('Whan that Aprill with his shoures soote', *General Prologue*, 1).

With certain verbs, the negative adverb *ne* is amalgamated into the verb itself (*nas* for *ne was*, *noot* for *ne woot*, *nadde* for *ne hadde*). A double negative does not, as in Modern English, make a positive, but negatives are multiplied for emphasis ('Hir frendshipe nas nat newe to biginne', *General Prologue*, 430; 'A bettre preest I trowe that nowher noon is', *General Prologue*, 526).

Pronouns

These are as in Modern English, with the following exceptions:
1st person singular: ich is used as well as *I*.

3rd person singular: there is no separate neuter form in the genitive, so that *his* is used for 'its'.

2nd person plural: ye in the nominative.

3rd person plural: for 'them' Chaucer uses *hem*, and for 'their' *hire* or *here*.

In Modern English the second person singular forms ('thou', etc.) are not normally used. In Chaucer's language, as in modern French or German, a person may be addressed either in the singular or in the plural, the singular indicating familiarity and the plural indicating respect. Thus, in *The Canterbury Tales*, the Host addresses the Prioress as *ye* because of her high social and spiritual standing, but calls the drunken Miller *thou*. Subtle changes in attitudes towards other people can thus sometimes be expressed simply through a change of number in the pronoun.

Relative pronouns are often followed by a *that* which would be redundant in Modern English (e.g. 'And eek in *what* array *that* they were inne', *General Prologue*, 41).

Verbs

Both strong and weak verbs are found, as in Modern English, but some verbs which are now weak were still strong in Chaucer's time. Thus *helpen*, 'to help', has as its past tense *holp* or *heelp* and as its past participle *holpen* ('That hem hath holpen whan that they were seeke', *General Prologue*, 18).

Present indicative. The third person singular is in *-eth* ('So priketh hem nature in hir corages', *General Prologue*, 11). The plural often ends in *-en* ('Thanne longen folk to goon on pilgrimages', *General Prologue*, 12).

Imperative. The plural, used to more than one person and also, for politeness, to a single person, often ends in *-eth* ('"Cometh neer", quod he, "my lady Prioresse"', *General Prologue*, 841).

Infinitive. This often ends in *-en* ('Redy to wenden on my pilgrimage', *General Prologue*, 21).

Past participle. This is often prefixed by *y-* ('For he was late ycome from his viage', *General Prologue*, 77).

As in Modern English, there are various special irregularities in verbs, and these will be noted in the glossaries of the separate Tales.

Vocabulary

Although, as we have seen, French was in Chaucer's time being displaced by English, the English that was displacing it was very different in vocabulary from the English of Anglo-Saxon times. It had acquired large numbers of new words from French itself, and also from Latin, and Chaucer makes great use of these. It is significant that in the second half of the fourteenth century more French words were adopted into English than in any other half-century from the Norman conquest to the present.[1] This French vocabulary covers particularly the fields of government and law, the Church, the arts, and social and domestic life—all the interests of the upper class who had earlier spoken French themselves. Borrowings from Latin belong largely to 'clerkly' matters—theology, the sciences, literature, and so on. These foreign elements form a very large part of Chaucer's language, though there is no reason to suppose that he was responsible for *introducing* many French or Latin words into English. It seems likely, however, that this learned element in his vocabulary was more striking to his contemporaries than it is to us, simply because many of the words which were novel when he used them

[1] See A. C. Baugh, *A History of the English Language*, 2nd edn. (London, 1959), pp. 213–15.

have now become familiar parts of the language. Certainly Chaucer's fifteenth-century imitators were particularly struck by his mastery of a learned style, full of 'aureate terms' remote from common usage. To his followers, indeed, he must have seemed rather as Milton seemed in the eighteenth century, one who had raised English to the level of more dignified tongues by the use of what the Scottish poet Dunbar admiringly called 'fresch anamalit termes celicall' (bright enamelled celestial terms). It must be added that, as a model for imitation, Chaucer seen in this light was as disastrously stifling as Milton later proved to be. Even in the fifteenth century, however, there were those who could also see Chaucer as one who 'wrytteth no voyde wordes' (Caxton, writing in about 1483). And now that the French and Latin elements in English have come to feel perfectly familiar, Chaucer's language appears to embody a miraculously successful synthesis of the native and the foreign. More will be said about this synthesis in ch. 5 below.

This is a convenient point to add a warning. Although a modern reader will recognize a very high proportion of Chaucer's words at a first glance, it must be remembered that in some cases a word will have remained the same even though its meaning has altered. Some particularly important words of this kind, representing some of the key elements in medieval thought, are discussed at length in the Appendix to this volume. There are many other examples, however, and they are particularly deceptive because the modern reader may simply not notice that he is misunderstanding Chaucer's language. Thus Chaucer's *sentence* means not 'sentence' but 'meaning' or 'opinion'. *Prisoun* may mean 'prison', but also sometimes 'prisoner'. *Wys* in such a phrase as 'For God so wys be my savacioun' (*Wife of Bath's Tale*, 621) means not 'wise' but 'surely'. *Dame* means not 'old woman' (as in a pantomime) nor yet 'girl' (as in American slang), but simply 'lady'. Provided one assumes that Chaucer is writing sense (as he invariably is), a close attention to his general train of thought will usually enable one to avoid such traps, and will take one a long way towards an understanding of his language.

Pronunciation

It is not difficult to learn to speak Chaucer's poetry roughly as it would have been pronounced in his own time. We cannot be sure, of course, of the exact details of English pronunciation six hundred years ago—still less of the details of intonation—but we can come somewhere near them. It is important to try to do so, because most of Chaucer's poetry was written to be spoken aloud (as *The Canterbury Tales* are spoken by the pilgrims), and for that very reason its sound carries a large part of its meaning. As a modern scholar has written, 'his best effects were auditory, as they were bound to be with one who was raised in a society where a minstrel or a reader-aloud, not a library, was the distributing agent for literature'.[1]

The greatest differences between twentieth- and fourteenth-century pronunciation are in the vowels, and one general principle to remember is that the medieval pronunciation of vowels was purer than our own. When we say 'note', the sound represented by the vowel *o* is in fact a diphthong in which the *o* sound gradually changes into an *oo* sound. In the fourteenth century it was still a pure *o*, and similarly with other vowels. Thus in the tables of modern equivalents to Chaucer's vowels given below, it must be remembered that the modern sound is sometimes only a rough equivalent to the fourteenth-century sound.

Short vowels

ă represents the sound now written *u*, as in 'cut'.

ĕ as in modern 'set'.

ĭ as in modern 'is'.

ŏ as in modern 'top'.

ŭ as in modern 'put' (not as in 'cut').

final *-e* represents the neutral vowel sound as in '*a*bout' or 'attenti*on*' (see below under Versification).

[1] E. T. Donaldson, *Publications of the Modern Language Association of America* (1948), 1121.

Long vowels

$\bar{a}$ roughly as in modern 'father', but more as in French *page* (not as in 'name')

$\bar{e}$ (open) roughly as in modern 'there' but more like *è* in French *père*.

$\bar{e}$ (close) as *é* in French *thé*, but long.

$\bar{\imath}$ as in 'machine' (not as in 'like').

$\bar{o}$ (open) represents the sound now written *aw*, as in 'fawn'.

$\bar{o}$ (close) as in French *gauche*.

$\bar{u}$ roughly as in modern 'duke', but more like French *tu*.

The difference between close $\bar{e}$ and $\bar{o}$ and open $\bar{e}$ and $\bar{o}$ is that the former are pronounced with higher tongue positions and greater tension than the latter; close $\bar{o}$ also has tighter lip-rounding than open $\bar{o}$. One can usually tell whether the close or open sound is the right one by reference to modern spelling and pronunciation. In a word where $\bar{e}$ is now spelt *e* or *ee* (as in 'we' or 'see') it should usually be pronounced close; where it is now spelt *ea* (as in 'team') it should usually be pronounced open. In a word where $\bar{o}$ is now pronounced like the *o* or *oo* in 'brother', 'mood' or 'good', it should be pronounced close; where it is now pronounced like the *o* or *oa* in 'rode' or 'road', it should be pronounced open.

Diphthongs

ai and *ei* both roughly represent the long sound now written *i* or *y* as in 'die' or 'dye'.

au and *aw* represent the sound now written *ou* or *ow*, as in 'pounce' or 'now'.

ou and *ow* have two pronunciations. If in the equivalent modern word these sounds are pronounced as in 'mouse' or 'through', the medieval pronunciation was as in 'through'. If in the equivalent modern word they are pronounced as in 'know' or 'thought', the medieval pronunciation was similar to that of the *au* or *aw* diphthong.

Spelling of vowels

Medieval spelling was probably more phonetic than modern spelling, but it was still by no means entirely regular. One fairly common habit was for a long vowel to be indicated by doubling, as in 'roote' or 'eek'. This doubling does not, as in modern English, affect the quality of the vowel, but only its length. Two of the other more important variations in the spelling of vowels are as follows:

The *ŭ* sound is sometimes represented by an *o*, as in the Chaucerian 'yong'.

The *au* sound is sometimes represented by an *a*, especially before *m* or *n* followed by some other consonant, as in the Chaucerian 'cha(u)mbre' or 'cha(u)nce'.

Consonants

These stood for much the same sounds as in modern English, except that *gh* (now usually silent, as in 'throu*gh*') was pronounced like the *ch* in Scottish 'lo*ch*'. A further main difference to be noticed is that many other consonants which are sometimes silent in modern English were still always pronounced in Chaucer's time.

g was pronounced before *n*, as in the Chaucerian 'gnacchen' ('to gnash'), but only at the beginning of a word.

k was pronounced before *n*, as in the Chaucerian 'knave' ('boy').

r was trilled more strongly than in modern English—so as to sound more like its modern Scottish pronunciation—and it was still pronounced after a vowel, where in modern English it is usually silent (as in 'bird' or 'score'). In such cases, by a process called metathesis, the *r* and the vowel may sometimes change places, so that we may find 'thirled' and 'thrilled', both meaning 'pierced'.

l was still pronounced before *f*, *k*, and *m* (as in 'folk').

w was pronounced before *r* (as in 'wrong').

Versification

The basic line of Chaucer's verse in nearly all *The Canterbury Tales* is the same as that of Shakespeare's blank verse or Pope's heroic couplets: the iambic pentameter or line consisting of five feet, each foot made up of an unstressed syllable followed by a stressed syllable. Thus:

$$\overset{\times}{\text{A}} \overset{/}{\text{Knight}} \overset{\times}{\text{ther}} \overset{/}{\text{was}}, \overset{\times}{\text{and}} \overset{/}{\text{that}} \overset{\times}{\text{a}} \overset{/}{\text{worthy}} \overset{\times}{\text{man}}.^{1}$$

But, as in Shakespeare or Pope, great variation is possible within this basic pattern: feet may be reversed, extra unstressed syllables may be added, and the result will be very different from the stiff regularity of the basic line. Indeed, it is often possible to hear, behind the five-foot pattern (borrowed from French or Italian), a different rhythm based on that of Old English alliterative verse, and consisting of two half-lines separated by a slight pause, and each containing two heavily stressed syllables. Again, Chaucer sometimes introduces a variation unknown to Pope and uncommon in Shakespeare, by omitting the first, unstressed, syllable of a line. Thus:

$$\overset{/}{\text{Lo}}, \overset{\times}{\text{how}} \overset{/}{\text{deere}}, \overset{\times}{\text{shortly}} \overset{/}{\text{for}} \overset{\times}{\text{to}} \overset{/}{\text{sayn}}.$$

Headless lines of this type, however, are the only ones likely to give any difficulty to someone accustomed to reading English verse. In reading Chaucer aloud, it is probably better not to attempt a mechanical division into feet and stressed and unstressed syllables, but simply to follow the natural rhythm of each phrase as it might be spoken, while at the same time keeping in mind the basic $\times / \times / \times / \times / \times /$ pattern. Like other English poets, Chaucer produces some of his most effective verse by playing off the actual rhythms of speech against the 'ideal' pattern of metrical regularity: the expectation of regularity is built up so that it may be defeated as well as fulfilled.

There remains one important point to be made clear, and this concerns the final *e* in words such as 'name', 'veine' and 'ende'. In modern English this is silent, and in the colloquial pronunciation of the London area in Chaucer's day it was probably ceasing to be sounded. The situation was so fluid that it seems to have been

---

[1] The symbol × is used to stand for an unstressed syllable, / for a strongly stressed syllable, and \ for a lightly stressed syllable. This notation can of course represent only very approximately the great variety of degrees of stress in English.

possible for Chaucer sometimes to retain the pronunciation of final *e* in his verse—so fully indeed that he can rhyme 'Rome' with 'to me'—and sometimes to drop it. The texts in the accompanying series have been constructed on the assumption that the final *e* ought still to be pronounced by the modern reader, *except* where the next word in the line begins with a vowel or an *h*. It will also be pronounced in the last word of a line and, of course, when a word ending in *e* in the singular is made plural (as in 'list*es*' or 'lokk*es*'). It must be emphasized, however, that the question of the pronunciation of final *e* cannot yet be regarded as settled.

Bearing these hints in mind, we may offer the following specimen of scansion, intended merely as a very rough guide to the rhythms of Chaucer's verse. (Silent final *e* is bracketed.)

> A yeerd she hadd(e), enclosed al aboute
> With stikkes, and a drye dich withoute,
> In which she hadd(e) a cok, hight Chauntecleer.
> In al the land, of crowing nas his peer.
> His voys was murier than the muri(e) orgon
> On messe-dayes that in the chirche gon.
> Wel sikerer was his crowing in his logge
> Than is a clokk(e) or an abbey orlogge.
> By nature he knew ech ascencioun
> Of th(e) equinoxial in thilke toun.[1]

Chaucer's rhetoric

Chaucer, and especially the mature Chaucer of *The Canterbury Tales*, has been most widely praised as the poet of human nature, the poet who has fixed forever in his Canterbury pilgrims the whole range of humanity as it really is. The praise is just. Dryden wrote, three centuries after Chaucer's death, that 'We have our forefathers and

---

[1] *The Nun's Priest's Tale*, ll. 81–90.

great-grand-dames all before us, as they were in Chaucer's days: their general characters are still remaining in mankind, and even in England, though they are called by other names than those of Monks, and Friars, and Canons, and Lady Abbesses, and Nuns';[1] and today, nearly three more centuries on, the English could still say the same. It would be easy to go on to assume that this poet *of* nature was also one who wrote *by* nature and not by art. The impression made by *The Canterbury Tales* not simply on ordinary modern readers but on literary scholars is (to quote one of the latter) that 'His English is plain, terse, homely, colloquial English, taken alive out of daily speech....He avoids all "counterfeited terms", all subtleties of rhetoric...'.[2] This, often enough, may be the impression that Chaucer strives to give; as when he makes the Franklin preface his Tale with the apology:

> I lerned nevere rethorik, certeyn;
> Thing that I speke, it moot be bare and pleyn.

Yet, if we think of this remark as being simply dramatically appropriate, and look at the Tale itself, we shall find that it is far from 'bare and pleyn'—it is in fact loaded with 'the subtleties of rhetoric'. The modern reader may be reluctant to believe this, because, since the great Romantics wrote—since Wordsworth declared that 'All good poetry is the spontaneous overflow of powerful feelings'— ordinary readers have tended to feel that spontaneity or 'naturalness' is a highly desirable quality in literature, so that the 'subtleties of rhetoric' are best avoided and the most genuine art is unpremeditated. This is most unlikely to have been Chaucer's own view. In the Middle Ages 'art' was conceived of as what we should call (perhaps disparagingly) craft or technique. At that time 'the dignity of art derived from its participation in an organized body of knowledge. The Middle Ages had no conception of an artist who was ignorant of the rules of his craft.' An anonymous twelfth-century writer

---

[1] *Of Dramatic Poesy and Other Critical Essays*, ed. George Watson (London, 1962), II, 284–5.

[2] Sir Walter Raleigh, *On Writing and Writers* (London, 1926), pp. 115–16.

defines an 'art' as 'a collection of precepts by which we are informed how to do something more easily than by nature'.[1] For Chaucer, there seems to have been no such distinction as modern readers might like to make between 'rethorik' and poetry. There existed in his time numerous textbooks on *ars poetica*, the art of poetry, and these were textbooks of the craft of rhetoric. Chaucer knew of this *ars poetica*, or, as he calls it in *The House of Fame*, 'art poetical'. There too his reference to this art is accompanied by a denial that he wishes to display it, but *The House of Fame* is nevertheless full of the devices taught by the art—devices which include, as it happens, the very formula of modesty exemplified in Chaucer's denial. Chaucer's 'art poetical' is conscious and elaborate, and precisely because of the modern prejudice in favour of the natural, which has caused 'artificial' and 'contrived' and 'rhetorical' to become terms of abuse, it will be worth our time to examine this 'art poetical' in some detail. In this way we shall notice the elements of contrivance and convention underlying effects that in themselves may seem perfectly 'natural'.

Rhetoric was taught in the Middle Ages as a regular part of the educational curriculum. It was one of the 'seven liberal arts', and if there had been a medieval School Certificate or General Certificate of Education it would undoubtedly have included rhetoric as one of the subjects examined, though perhaps only at Advanced level. After the medieval student had learnt 'grammar', which included far more then than it does now—understanding the meaning of Latin texts and writing and speaking Latin correctly—he passed on to 'rhetoric', which taught the rules for composing literature oneself, again in Latin. There existed a large number of works intended as textbooks for the teaching of rhetoric in this sense, and these are known as the *artes poeticae*. Most of these works were composed in the earlier Middle Ages, and their teachings were not original, but derived from classical Latin treatises on rhetoric, including works by

---

[1] Both the preceding quotations are from E. de Bruyne, *Études d'esthétique médiévale* (Bruges, 1946), II, 374 and 372.

Cicero and Horace and one, the *Rhetorica ad Herennium*, which in the Middle Ages was attributed to Cicero, though it is not now thought to be by him. In *The Nun's Priest's Tale* Chaucer actually refers to one of the medieval authors of *artes poeticae* by name, and it may be interesting to pause for a moment over this reference. The context is that the cock Chauntecleer has been tricked by a fox into closing his eyes and stretching out his neck in order to sing better. The fox immediately seizes Chauntecleer and makes off with him, obviously intending to carry him back to his hole and there eat him. All this has occurred on a Friday. At this exciting point in his narrative the Nun's Priest pauses to insert three invocations: first of destiny, second of Venus (whose day Friday is, and whose diligent servant Chauntecleer was, since he had seven wives), and third of 'Gaufred, deere maister soverain'—

> That whan thy worthy king Richard was slain
> With shot, compleynedest[1] his deeth so soore,
> Why ne hadde I now thy sentence and thy loore,[2]
> The Friday for to chide, as diden ye?
> For on a Friday, soothly, slain was he.
> Thanne wolde I shewe yow how that I koude pleyne
> For Chauntecleres drede and for his peyne.

'Gaufred' is Geoffroi de Vinsauf, who wrote an *ars poetica* called the *Poetria nova* (New Poetry). One of the rhetorical devices he recommends is *exclamatio*, defined by the *Ad Herennium* as 'the figure which expresses grief or indignation by means of an address to some man or city or place or object'.[3] Geoffroi gives several examples of it, among them a lamentation on the death of King Richard I, which includes an address to Friday, the day on which this misfortune, like Chauntecleer's, occurred. The effect of Chaucer's reference is thus doubly comic: it applies this grandly emotional device to the misfortune of a mere farmyard animal, and it also brings out the absurdity inherent in the very idea of a solemn address to one of the

---

[1] 'lamented'. [2] 'learning'.

[3] *Rhetorica ad Herennium*, ed. Harry Caplan (London, 1954), p. 283.

days of the week. Clearly Geoffroi is not being treated with much respect, but this cannot be taken to mean that Chaucer despised the *ars poetica* itself. He treats Geoffroi with just the affectionate derision that a middle-aged man might be expected to feel for a textbook from his schooldays: one might make fun of Hussey, Spearing and Winny without despising English literature. Chaucer could afford to laugh at the textbook precisely because he knew so well what it had taught him. His works are full of the rhetorical devices that Geoffroi teaches, used sometimes, as in *The Nun's Priest's Tale*, for comic effect, but more often with perfect seriousness.[1]

Chaucer, then, seems to have been familiar with the *artes poeticae*. What could he have learned from them? About the structure of literary works he could have learned very little, for this is a subject on which they have little to say. They explain how to begin a poem, in a way which avoids jumping straight into the narrative: with a story illustrating some more general point (an *exemplum*) or with a statement of some general truth about life (a *sententia*). Chaucer often chooses the second method. Thus the Prioress, before she can begin on the actual events of her story—

> Ther was in Asye, in a greet citee,
> Amonges Cristene folk, a Jewerye...

—must introduce it with a prologue beginning

> O Lord, oure Lord, thy name how merveillous
> Is in this large world ysprad....

If one begins in this way, the *artes poeticae* explain, it is necessary to link one's initial generalities somehow with one's actual story; and so, in *Troilus and Criseyde*, after Chaucer has written some fifty

---

[1] It has recently been argued (J. J. Murphy, 'A New Look at Chaucer and the Rhetoricians', *Review of English Studies*, 1964) that Chaucer may not have read the *artes poeticae* themselves, and that he could have come upon Geoffroi's lamentation on Richard I in a form detached from the *Poetria nova*. The matter cannot be taken as proved either way; and in any case there can be no doubt that Chaucer could have found the essential teaching of the *artes poeticae* in medieval encyclopaedias and in works on 'grammar'.

lines of opening invocation, he returns to begin the real story by
saying

> Now herkneth with a good entencioun,
> For now wil I gon streght to my matere.

The *artes poeticae* also explain how to bring one's work to an end;
and that is about all the help they offer with structure.

Their main interest is not in the overall organization of a poem but
in the more detailed techniques of literature. Geoffroi takes these
up by assuming two possible purposes that they may serve: to
extend one's material (*amplificatio*) and to abridge it (*abbreviatio*).
Chaucer interestingly shows his awareness of this basic assumption
in some lines in *Troilus and Criseyde*, where he offers what he has
written for correction by those who have more experience of love
than he has,

> To encresse or maken diminucioun
> Of my langage....

Geoffroi's formula helps to bring out an underlying postulate of the
medieval art of poetry, a postulate that was certainly held by Chaucer
himself. This is that the poet's business was not to invent new stories
but to retell old stories in a new way, perhaps so as to make them
serve some purpose of his own. Thus the stories in *The Legend of
Good Women* are taken from a variety of sources, but are retold in
such a way that they all illustrate the martyrdom of women in love.
For us, to call a writer 'original' is to give him the highest praise; in
the Middle Ages, if the word had existed in our sense (significantly,
it did not) the very reverse would have been true. Chaucer, like all
medieval writers, boasts not of the originality of his material but of
its age and authenticity. Thus *The Knight's Tale*, for example,
begins:

> Whilom, *as olde stories tellen us*,
> Ther was a duc that highte Theseus....

Chaucer's main source in *The Knight's Tale* is the *Teseida* of
Boccaccio, and Boccaccio in turn borrowed his story from earlier
writers. *The Knight's Tale* does not *mean* the same as any of these

'olde stories'—it expresses an 'original' and distinctively Chaucerian version of life—but for the Knight and for Chaucer it is important that this 'originality' should be firmly based on something traditional. Sometimes Chaucer will refer to the actual source of a story. The Clerk tells the pilgrims that he has his Tale from 'Fraunceys Petrak', an Italian poet famous for his 'rethorike', and goes on to offer some literary criticism of this source which nicely illustrates the ideas just mentioned on how to begin a story in an artistic way. He says that Petrarch began his Tale with a Prologue describing Italy; this was written in 'heigh stile', but its purpose was simply to 'conveyen his mateere' (introduce his subject), and so the Clerk proposes to omit it.

Of the two processes of amplification and abbreviation, Chaucer, like most medieval poets, makes most use of the former; partly, no doubt, because one needs extra space to reshape an existing work to a new purpose, and partly because for a medieval audience literature was essentially a pastime, and (like a modern television serial), the more time it could be extended to fill, the better. Chaucer does sometimes abbreviate, though, especially when setting the scene for a story: for example, he begins the actual narrative of *Troilus and Criseyde*, after the preliminaries mentioned above, with a masterly one-sentence summary of the course and purpose of the Trojan War:

> It is wel wist how that the Grekes, stronge
> In armes, with a thousand shippes, wente
> To Troiewardes, and the cite longe
> Assegeden,[1] neigh ten yer er they stente,[2]
> And in diverse wise and oon entente—
> The ravisshing to wreken[3] of Eleyne,
> By Paris don—they wroughten al hir peyne.

The *artes poeticae* describe and illustrate innumerable means of amplification, most of which Chaucer uses in one place or another. It would not be possible, even if it were desirable, to discuss all of them here, but a few examples will help to show what he could have

---

[1] 'Besieged'. [2] 'gave up'. [3] 'avenge'.

learned from them. We have already seen from *The Nun's Priest's Tale* how a work may be amplified through *exclamatio*. Comparisons form another way of amplifying material, and the *artes poeticae* encourage long ones which go beyond a mere simile. In *The Knight's Tale* Arcite pauses in his argument that human beings are blind in their wishes to add an illustrative comparison with a drunkard:

> We witen nat what thing we preyen heere:
> We faren as he that dronke is as a mous.
> A dronke man woot wel he hath an hous,
> But he noot which the righte wey is thider,
> And to a dronke man the wey is slider.
> And certes, in this world so faren we;
> We seken faste after felicitee,
> But we goon wrong ful often, trewely.

A simple idea may be extended by circumlocution. The Franklin does this in his Tale, and then calls our attention to it by explaining what he really means:

> Til that the brighte sonne loste his hewe;
> For th'orisonte hath reft the sonne his light,—[1]
> This is as muche to seye as it was night.

One may amplify material by making something inanimate speak as if it were human (*prosopopoeia*). The Physician begins his Tale by telling us of a knight who had an only child, a daughter so beautiful that she was Nature's masterpiece, and then he makes Nature herself amplify this idea:

> For Nature hath with soverein diligence
> Yformed hire in so greet excellence,
> As though she wolde seyn, 'Lo! I, Nature,
> Thus kan I forme and peynte a creature,
> Whan that me list; who kan me countrefete?'

Nature continues for another dozen lines, and then the Physician concludes the *prosopopoeia* by remarking, 'Thus semeth me that Nature wolde seye'. Another way of amplifying material is with descriptions, and this device was a favourite with Chaucer and other

---

[1] 'For the horizon had deprived the sun of his light'.

medieval poets. Medieval writers had a particularly keen eye for the outward appearance of things, and their works are full of minute descriptions, in which every detail is enumerated. We can find in Chaucer elaborate descriptions of people (especially women), of landscapes (especially gardens), of feasts and other ceremonies, of buildings (a particularly striking example being the temples of Mars, Venus, and Diana in *The Knight's Tale*), and other things. The *artes poeticae* prescribe both the method of description and something of its content. Thus in describing a beautiful lady one must first go through her features one by one, and these features will tend to include golden hair, white forehead, black eyebrows, and so on. Even when Chaucer purports to be describing a particular woman, as in *The Book of the Duchess*, where a lady is described who is clearly intended to represent the recently deceased Duchess of Lancaster, the description is of this rhetorical ideal rather than of an individual. And even where he seems to be *creating* an entirely new person, as in the descriptions in *The General Prologue*, or the Miller's utterly convincing description of the delicious young wife Alisoun, he still follows the enumerative method and retains some vestiges of the details the *artes poeticae* prescribe. With a person, the description of outward appearance (*effictio*) may be completed by a description of inward moral qualities (*notatio*). We find this in *The Physician's Tale*, where, after a brief description of the beautiful daughter's complexion and hair, there occur the transitional lines

> And if that excellent was hire beautee,
> A thousand foold moore vertuous was she

followed by a much longer list of her virtues. A means of amplification which may include almost any of the others mentioned, but especially description, is digression. In this the writer seems to turn away from the point he has reached in his chosen material, either to some other part of this material, or to something completely outside it. But the divergence must be only apparent, for, as Geoffroi warns the intending poet, digression must be relevant to the subject in hand. In *The Man of Law's Tale*, Custance has been falsely accused of murdering her host's wife. She prays to God to save her, and then suddenly, without any explanation or transition, the narrator turns to what seems a quite different subject:

> Have ye nat seyn somtime a pale face,
> Among a prees,[1] of him that hath be lad[2]
> Toward his deeth, wher as him gat no grace,
> And swich a colour in his face hath had,
> Men mighte knowe his face that was bistad,[3]
> Amonges alle the faces in that route?

What can this burningly vivid glimpse of something that Chaucer might well really have seen have to do with Custance? The next line makes it clear that the digression is really a simile: 'So stant Custance, and looketh hire about'.

Besides these and other means of amplifying a whole work, the *artes poeticae* also discuss, at even greater length, ways of ornamenting literary style in detail. These include 'tropes', many of which are so familiar that we need not pause over them—metaphor, synecdoche, hyperbole, and so on. One 'trope' which Chaucer can use with great effect is onomatopoeia, the imitation of meaning through sound. In *The Pardoner's Tale*, for example, when the Pardoner is denouncing gluttony, he explains how cooks even knock the marrow out of bones, because they waste nothing 'That may go thurgh the golet softe and swoote'—and that slippery-sounding line conveys with repulsive exactness the sense of swallowing something soft. There are also 'figures of thought', which include smaller-scale examples of many of the means of amplification already mentioned, and also such devices as understatement and antithesis, which are found naturally in any speech or writing. One favourite 'figure of thought' of Chaucer's is *exemplum*, the citing of a particular story which exemplifies the general point under discussion, and so makes it more vivid or more plausible. Chaucer's works are full of *exempla*, often taken from named writers, and thus adding authority as well as vividness to the point at issue. The Wife of Bath takes up the

---

[1] 'crowd'.   [2] 'led'.   [3] 'endangered'.

question (raised in her Tale) of what thing it is that women most desire. Some claim, she says, that women desire to be reliable and discreet, but that is not true: 'Pardee, we wommen konne no thing hele'. To make this assertion more convincing, she adds, 'Witnesse on Mida,—wol ye heere the tale?' and goes on to tell the story of Midas, and how his wife could not keep to herself the fact that he had ass's ears. This is taken from Ovid; and after nearly thirty lines of it, the Wife concludes by again relating the *exemplum* to its original context:

> Heere may ye se, thogh we a time abide,
> Yet out it moot; we kan no conseil hide.
> The remenant of the tale if ye wol heere,
> Redeth Ovide, and ther ye may it leere.

The Franklin's Tale at one place includes twenty-one *exempla* in succession, all illustrating the assertion that many women have killed themselves rather than submit to dishonour. The Physician, on the other hand, after giving a single *exemplum* to show that innocence must be protected, remarks

> Suffiseth oon ensample now as heere,
> For I moot turne again to my matere.

Beside the 'tropes' and 'figures of thought', the *artes poeticae* describe finally the 'figures of words'. These are devices involving the arrangement of words rather than their meaning. There are, for example, different kinds of repetition: repetition of the same words at the beginning of a series of phrases—

> 'Phebus', quod he, '*for al thy* worthinesse,
> *For al thy* beautee and thy gentilesse,
> *For al thy* song and al thy minstralcye,
> *For al thy* waiting, blered is thyn ye.'[1]

—or at the end, or at both beginning and end; or a repetition of different grammatical forms of the same root-word:

> And he that wole han pris[2] of his *gentrye*,
> For he was boren of a *gentil* hous,
> And hadde his eldres noble and vertuous,

---

[1] 'you have been hoodwinked' (from *The Maniple's Tale*).　　　[2] 'be valued for'.

> And nel himselven do no *gentil* dedis,
> Ne folwen his *gentil* auncestre that deed is,
> He nis nat *gentil*, be he duc or erl;
> For vileyns sinful dedes make a cherl.
> For *gentillesse* nis but renomee[1]
> Of thyne auncestres....[2]

Among figures of words Geoffroi also includes some devices that might be better classified differently—his classification is not particularly systematic. One of these, which Chaucer frequently uses, is *occupatio*, the refusal to say something one might say. This may be employed as a suggestive form of abbreviation, as when the Knight declines to speculate about the destination of Arcite's soul—

> His spirit chaunged hous and wente ther,
> As I cam nevere, I kan nat tellen wher.
> Therfore I stinte, I nam no divinistre;
> Of soules finde I nat in this registre,
> Ne me ne list thilke opinions to telle
> Of hem, though that they writen wher they dwelle.

—or as a way of mentioning something even while refusing to mention it, as when he spends forty-six lines refusing to describe every detail of Arcite's funeral.

Some of the rhetorical techniques we have been glancing at are clearly used by Chaucer consciously and deliberately. One could hardly extend a refusal to describe in such a way as to turn it into a detailed description without noticing what one was doing. Others might appear in everyday speech, in Chaucer's time or in ours, as the natural expressions of feeling—and this would apply even to certain elaborate figures, such as rhetorical questions. But in either case, it may now be asked what interest this rhetorical armoury of Chaucer's has for the modern reader. One main interest has already been suggested. Once we become aware of Chaucer's 'art poetical', we gain a deeper insight into his work by seeing how what appears natural in it is in fact achieved not carelessly but by the play of genius upon convention and contrivance. It has been suggested

---

[1] 'renown'.   [2] *The Wife of Bath's Tale.*

that the process of Chaucer's literary career is one of gradual liberation from this 'art poetical', liberation from art into life, but this is surely a mistaken view. Chaucer learns to make better use of his rhetoric, learns to make it serve his expressive purpose more completely, but he never abandons it. And making better use of rhetoric does not necessarily mean concealing it. Chaucer's verbal art sometimes conceals itself, certainly, and sometimes makes fun of itself, but it also displays itself sometimes, in the pride of conscious mastery over difficult material. In doing so it provides a release from (what indeed Chaucer never aimed at) 'the desert of exact likeness to the reality which is perceived by the most commonplace mind'.[1] There are many passages in Chaucer which are 'natural' in the sense that they provide exactly the thoughts and feelings which the occasion demands, but which are 'artificial' in the sense that in real life such full and precise expression would never have been achieved. Chaucer's study of rhetoric helped him to write such passages. Finally, it must be added that he wrote them for the living voice and ear, rather than the dead page. This applies particularly to the 'figures of words'. They are part of an *oral* rhetoric, a rhetoric which conveys meaning through sound far more than we are accustomed to in post-medieval literature. Chaucer's repetitions and variations may sometimes seem obtrusive and tedious to the scholar in his study, but when they are heard they spring to life again, and their function in transmitting emotion becomes clear.

[1] T. S. Eliot, *Selected Essays* (London, 1934), p. 111.

5. CHAUCER THE WRITER

What appears to be Chaucer's earliest surviving poem is a translation; and this fact is so far from being a matter of chance that we may almost take it as symbolic. The poem is a prayer to the Virgin Mary, called *An ABC* because the initial letters of the successive stanzas form an alphabet, and it is taken from the French of Guillaume Deguilleville. Chaucer probably translated it when he was in his twenties, for presentation to Blanche, duchess of Lancaster, and it contains nothing that one would think of as characteristically Chaucerian. It is just the kind of impersonal exercise in religious and verbal ingenuity that any medieval court-poet might have written for any devout and noble patroness. Certainly it is entirely lacking in that intimately personal flavour that seems characteristic even of Chaucer's most dignified later poems—that sense of an ever-present yet ever-elusive Chaucerian narrator and commentator. And yet in its style *An ABC* already points towards one of the most important elements in Chaucer's achievement. From the opening lines we see a large proportion of its words are derived from Latin:

> Almighty and al merciable queene,
> To whom that al this world fleeth for socour,
> To have relees of sinne, of sorwe, and teene,
> Glorious virgine, of alle floures flour,
> To thee I flee, confounded in errour.

These Latinate words came to Chaucer through French; and Latin, French, and also Italian, already possessed literatures of a more developed kind than England had when Chaucer wrote them. One of Chaucer's main tasks, throughout his literary career, was to make the achievements of these literatures available in English. On the level of style, for instance, we can see him even in this early and very minor poem borrowing from Latin and French an idiom which was not native to English: a flowing, resonant, and dignified style, remote from everyday speech and full of abstractions, highly suitable for a public address to the Blessed Virgin. Even here, though, where the style is not distinctively Chaucerian, it is at least recognizably English, not simply a translator's jargon. We find the native 'almighty' paired and even alliterating with the Romance 'al merciable'; the Romance 'relees' is followed by a trio of familiar English words, 'sinne', 'sorwe' and 'teene'. The 'high style' of the original has been at least partly naturalized. In his later poems Chaucer achieves a complete naturalization, a style in which he absorbs Ovid or Guillaume de Lorris or Boccaccio, changes them, and is changed by them. He constantly translates, but in translating he transmutes: he recreates his original as something new, something distinctively English and distinctively Chaucerian. In his own lifetime, Chaucer was referred to by his French contemporary Eustache Deschamps as 'grant translateur', and he was, of course, a translator of something more than continental *styles* into English, and of something more than the bare doctrine of those he translated. He translated their sensibility, their whole *mode* of thinking and feeling, and recreated that too in doing so; and this is true whether he remade a complete work (as in *Troilus and Criseyde*), or whether he incorporated passages borrowed from other authors into structures of his own. If we understand translation not simply as a word-for-word process (though Chaucer sometimes used that too, as in his prose version of Boethius's *De Consolatione Philosophiae*) but as a matter of the absorption and recreation of literary traditions and sensibilities, then Chaucer is often at his most original as a translator.

Chaucer's earliest poems bring into English a French literary tradition. Medieval French literature had reached its peak long before Chaucer's lifetime: in epic, in the *Chanson de Roland* (eleventh century), and in chivalric romance, in the works of Chrétien de Troyes (twelfth century). It is doubtful whether Chaucer, writing in completely changed social conditions, would have found epic poetry at all useable. In Chrétien, on the other hand, he would have discovered a delightful play of fancy, a picture of aristocratic manners, a keen and often humorous perception of human psychology (especially in matters of love), and even, on occasion, a realism of description, all of which he might have found congenial and put to good use. But there are no signs that Chaucer knew of this earlier flowering of French literature. He was most widely read in, and most influenced by, the thinner and more decadent French writers current in the English court of his own day—Guillaume de Machaut, Jean Froissart, Eustache Deschamps, and others. Their typical literary form is the dream-allegory, and their concern is not with the world of common experience, the world of physical and psychological adventure, so much as with the systems and abstractions of the art of love as this was formalized in medieval courtly society. A modern reader may wish that the young Chaucer had found better models; but tastes change, and Chaucer in his time found much to engage his interest in works that now seem tedious. Besides, he also knew extremely well one earlier French work of far greater interest, which lay behind the whole tradition of dream-allegory. This is the *Roman de la Rose*, which was begun early in the thirteenth century by Guillaume de Lorris, and completed some forty years later by Jean de Meun. Guillaume began with a dream of a beautiful garden of love, in which a young man learns from experience the pleasures and pains of conducting a courtly love affair. Jean's continuation—four times as long as what it continues—develops the ironies inherent in the original with such relish and fertility that it has seemed to many readers to be written in an entirely different spirit.

In *The Legend of Good Women* Chaucer lists a translation of the *Roman de la Rose* among his own works, and there exists a Middle English translation of part of the poem which was for long printed among his works. Modern scholars hesitate to attribute to Chaucer more than the first fragment of this version, and if this fragment is by him it is presumably among his earliest works. It is a comparatively literal translation, which reproduces the octosyllabic couplets of the French, and transmits very exactly Guillaume's ideal dream-world,

its bright clear May morning through which a young and uncritical Dreamer wanders in leisure to learn about the art of love.
The dream-world is the real world of medieval leisure-class existence
idealized and distanced—a garden cut off from the troubles of everyday reality, and full of running streams, bright flowers, and singing
birds. From this garden are excluded the sins, and also such unpleas-
ing elements of human life as grief, old age, and poverty. These
appear only as grotesque figures painted on the garden wall. The
poem is at once didactic and ironic: through a drama of personifications it teaches 'al the art of love', the proper way of conducting a
love affair according to the customs of courtly society, yet at the same
time it presents love as sickness, folly, irrationality, no more than a
parody of the love of God. The Dreamer's guide is Idelnesse, a
young lady such as one might see nowadays photographed in *Vogue*:

> She hadde no thought, by night ne day,
> Of nothing, but if it were oonly
> To graythe hir[1] wel and uncouthly.

The lord of the garden is Mirthe, and among his friends inside it are
Beaute, Richesse (significantly juxtaposed: 'Biside Beaute yede
Richesse'), Youthe, and the God of Love himself:

> ...on his heed was set
> Of roses reed a chapelett.
> But nightingales, a ful gret route,
> That flyen over his heed aboute,
> The leeves felden as they flyen;
> And he was al with briddes wryen.[2]

Here personification is enlarged into myth. Beside the well where
Narcissus died of love for his own reflexion, the Dreamer sees a rose-
bush, is shot by an arrow from the God of Love's bow, and falls in
love with a symbolic rose-bud. And so the affair begins; we need
follow it no further. *The Romaunt of the Rose* carries across from the
French an unforgettable evocation of a seeming paradise of eternal
youth and beauty, and within this setting a doctrine of secular love.
Love remained one of Chaucer's main subjects throughout his

---

[1] 'array herself'.   [2] 'covered'.

career, and in this he is typical of his period. It is characteristic of
the Middle Ages to set love, human or divine, at the centre of their
view of the world.

Chaucer's first major original work also belongs to the tradition of
erotic dream-allegory. This is *The Book of the Duchess*, a poem on
the death of the lady Blanche for whom *An ABC* had been written,
and composed presumably to console her husband. In it the paradisal dream-world of *The Romaunt of the Rose* reappears. The
Dreamer dreams of waking up on another May morning in a bed-
room where

> ...alle the walles with colours fine
> Were peynted, bothe texte and glose,[1]
> Of al the Romaunce of the Rose.

But now, at the heart of the ideal landscape, the Dreamer finds
tragedy: a young knight dressed in black who, as he discovers by a
series of questions, is in mourning for his dead lady, 'goode faire
White'. 'White' is of course Blanche anglicized, and the knight
stands for the Duke of Lancaster, John of Gaunt. But the Dreamer's
conversation with the knight is preceded by a complicated sequence
of preliminaries. The narrator first explains how he had been
reduced to insomnia by unrequited love, then how he read a book to
pass away the night. The book was evidently Ovid's *Metamorphoses*,
a favourite source of stories for medieval writers, and one that was
current in a 'moralized' French version as well as in the original
Latin. In it he read how King 'Seys' (Ceyx) was drowned on a
voyage, and how his wife 'Alcione' (Alcyone) prayed to Juno for a
vision of him. Juno ordered Morpheus, the god of sleep, to send
Alcyone a dream of her dead husband, and when Ceyx explained in
the dream that he was drowned, his wife died too, of grief. The
narrator then himself prays to Morpheus to send him sleep, promising him the gift of a feather bed if he does so. His prayer is answered,
he sleeps, and his dream begins. But still the poem's chief subject
does appear. The Dreamer hears the noises of a hunt; he sees the
huntsmen pursuing a hart, is led deep into a forest by a little puppy,

---

[1] 'commentary'.

and only then comes upon the man in black and embarks on the long dialogue about his lady, from which it emerges at last that she is dead. Then the Dreamer wakes up again, and the poem is over.

In subject-matter *The Book of the Duchess* appears both miscellaneous and derivative. Chaucer is once again borrowing from the French, but he is now not translating a single poem literally, but combining material from Ovid, from the *Roman de la Rose*, from Froissart, and from several poems by Machaut. Yet this variety of material is almost completely remade into a Chaucerian whole. The 'wholeness' of *The Book of the Duchess* may seem doubtful, yet a strange unity underlies its disordered surface. The story of Ceyx and Alcyone is about a happily married couple parted by the death of the husband, and about a dream; it is followed by an actual dream, in which we learn of another couple also parted by death, this time that of the wife—a mirror image of the Ovidian situation. The Dreamer first sees huntsmen and hounds pursuing a hart; then, following a miniature hound, the puppy, he embarks on a hunt of his own, 'stalks' (his own word) the man in black, and seeks out the heart of that Hamlet-like figure's mystery. That there is a pun on 'hart' and 'heart' is suggested by the fact that both hunts end simultaneously: the man in black announces that the cause of his grief is his lady's death,

> And with that word right anoon
> They gan to strake forth; al was doon,
> For that time, the hert-hunting.

Thus we can find in *The Book of the Duchess* those strange associative links that underlie the confusion of dreams in real life. In the *Roman*, and in Chaucer's other French sources in this poem, the dream was only a conventional starting-handle for a poem, but he has now followed the actual processes of dreaming to produce a radically new kind of literary structure. In doing so, he has at least partly turned his material into something recognizably Chaucerian. The Chaucerian quality of *The Book of the Duchess* centres in its narrator. In the *Roman* we are scarcely aware of the Dreamer himself, except as an innocent and enthusiastic 'eye'; in the *Book*, under the influence of Machaut's work, this innocence becomes a more positive quality of character, and the Dreamer forces himself on our attention as a naïve and childlike fellow, literal-minded, clumsy, and ill at ease in the ideal world of his dream. He fails to understand the elegant love and aristocratic grief of the man in black, and can console him only indirectly by asking blundering questions which provoke him to give words to his sorrow.

Clearly this Dreamer cannot be identical with the intelligent poet who created him, even though that poet refers to him as 'I'. He is only a mask for Chaucer himself, and in inventing this mask Chaucer has begun to develop one of his most important poetic devices. In all his subsequent major poetry Chaucer conceals himself behind a similarly naïve narrator. The idiot-dreamer of *The Book of the Duchess* develops into the idiot-historian of *Troilus and Criseyde* and the idiot-pilgrim of *The Canterbury Tales*. He is the means by which a comic irony is allowed to play on the most serious subject-matter, and by which the poem's listeners can be incited to supply from their own experience observations which the narrator notice-ably fails to make. In *The Book of the Duchess* a comedy radiates from the Dreamer which mingles with the poem's main tone of pathos with surprising success. By his obstinate refusal to accept a total idealization of Blanche, he strikes a convincingly human indignation from the man in black:

> 'By oure Lord', quod I, 'I trowe yow wel!
> Hardely, your love was wel beset;
> I not how ye mighte have do bet.'
> 'Bet? ne no wight so wel', quod he.
> 'I trowe hit, sir', quod I, 'parde!'
> 'Nay, leve hit wel!' 'Sire, so do I;
> I leve yow wel, that trewely
> Yow thoghte that she was the beste,
> And to beholde the alderfaireste,
> Whoso had loked with your eyen.'
> 'With myn? nay, alle that hir seyen
> Seyde and sworen hit was soo.'

For this comic realism in the dream itself we have been prepared by similar touches of comedy in the narrator's retelling of the story from Ovid: as in the scene where Juno's messenger bursts impatiently into the cave of Morpheus, and has some difficulty in gaining attention:

> This messenger com fleinge faste
> And cried, 'O, ho! awake anoon!'
> Hit was for noght; there herde him non.
> 'Awake!' quod he, 'whoo is lyth there?'
> And blew his horn right in here eere,
> And cried, 'Awaketh!' wonder hye.
> This god of slep, with his oon ye
> Cast up, axed, 'Who clepeth ther?'
> 'Hit am I', quod this messenger.

These comic touches are not out of place in a poem written to console the duke of Lancaster for his wife's death. They are associated so firmly with the Dreamer as to emphasize the distance between his everyday (and, as one might say, bourgeois) standards of judgement and the man in black's transcendentally aristocratic grief; and yet by being in the same poem they may serve to recall the duke to the human variety of the life that has still to be lived. *The Book of the Duchess* is not an entirely successful poem. Its stiffly idealized rendering of courtly love and courtly grief is only occasionally brought into contact with the more intimately known humanity of the Dreamer, and thus is largely shielded from the reader's free judgement. But it remains the poem in which Chaucer first transmuted continental sources into something recognizably his own, and a work whose experimental quality still communicates real excitement.

Chaucer's next work in the dream-allegory tradition, *The House of Fame*, pushes further many of the tendencies shown in *The Book of the Duchess*. It treats foreign sources still more freely, possesses an even more daringly centrifugal structure, and has a yet stronger personal flavour. It once again borrows from Chaucer's French contemporaries—Froissart and Nicole de Margival—but their influence is modified not only by that of Ovid and Virgil, but also by the first signs of Chaucer's reading in another continental literature, Italian. The major period of medieval Italian literature was nearer to Chaucer's own time than the major period of French, and he knew the work of three great Italian poets—Boccaccio, Petrarch and Dante. He seems to have read them for the first time during or after his trip to Italy in 1372, and he presumably brought manuscripts of their works back with him. In any case, from this time on his serious work is pervaded by their influence, and he knew them deeply enough to weave together almost instinctively allusions to different parts of their works. The Italian influence in *The House of Fame* is that of Dante, and it does not appear until the very end of book I of the poem; it has been suggested that Chaucer read Dante for the first time between finishing his first draft of book I and beginning book II.

In *The House of Fame* the opening of the dream is not delayed as it is in *The Book of the Duchess*, but once it has begun there are similar delays before the poem reaches its main subject. The Dreamer wakes up in a temple of glass dedicated to Venus. On its walls is depicted the story of the *Aeneid*, and Chaucer pauses to retell this, with particular emphasis on the love affair of Aeneas and Dido, until nearly the end of the first book. For the Middle Ages Virgil was the supreme Latin poet—Dante calls him the 'glory and light of other poets'—but his work was often completely re-interpreted, and the emphasis on the love-element in the *Aeneid* is typically medieval. Indeed, the *Aeneid* had been rewritten as a French chivalric romance, and Chaucer probably knew this as well as Virgil's own work. After this, the Dreamer walks out of the temple and finds himself in a desert, with a golden eagle swooping down on him from above. The eagle derives from canto IX of Dante's *Purgatorio*. In book II it seizes the Dreamer in its claws and flies away with him. They have a long conversation in mid-air, in which the eagle informs the Dreamer that Jove, to compensate him for his service to love (service of a purely literary kind, for he has had no practical success), is sending him to the House of Fame, where he will learn tidings of lovers all over the world. The eagle explains the theory of sound, so that the Dreamer may understand how information reaches Fame, and offers to explain astronomy to him too; but the Dreamer says he is too old to learn. In book III, the Dreamer, now abandoned by his guide, sees first a rock of ice with the names of famous people carved in it, some melted away and some still fresh; then a castle, its pinnacles covered with minstrels and magicians; and then, inside the castle, the hall of Fame, with the goddess herself enthroned in it. Around her are pillars with the great poets of the world standing on them. People come to her demanding or refusing fame, and she deals out good reputation, bad reputation, and oblivion not according to their deserts or wishes, but quite indiscriminately. The Dreamer is now accosted by an unnamed person, to whom he complains that he has not yet received the 'tidinges' he was promised. He is led to an enormous revolving house made of twigs and full of noise; and on this the eagle is perching. The eagle carries him into the wicker house, and there he finds companies of people whispering news to each other, and adding to it in the process; and the news flies out of the windows to the earth. He hears a noise in one corner, everyone begins running; at last he sees someone who

> ...semed for to be
> A man of gret auctorite.

At this point the poem breaks off, unfinished.

It seems unlikely that Chaucer could ever have finished it—unlikely that he could have found anything for the 'man of gret auctorite' to say that would have given the poem any overall meaning. In *The House of Fame* Chaucer has intensified the associative movement of *The Book of the Duchess* so far as to deprive the work of all unity. It is true that certain themes recur throughout the poem. Venus, the mother of Aeneas, is the presiding spirit of the Virgilian sequence in book I, and so it can be no surprise when the Dreamer finds himself in a temple dedicated to Venus in book II. And there runs throughout a general connexion between Love and

Fame: it is assumed that in the House of Fame the Dreamer will learn tidings of love. Humour is a more persistent element than in *The Book of the Duchess*, and, as there, it centres in the characterization of the Dreamer. This Dreamer is now more closely connected with the poet in some ways—he is called Geoffrey, and he shares Chaucer's labours as a customs official—but he is also more consistently separated from the real poet, and presented as a figure comically bewildered by the unfamiliar world of his dream. He is in a permanent attitude of ineffectual protest against the course the poem is taking, and his dialogue with the eagle in particular is a comic masterpiece. The eagle is no longer simply, like the man in black, an authoritative figure whom the Dreamer fails to understand, but a garrulous pedant whom he does not *wish* to understand. And so on one part we find complacent self-congratulation, and on the other monosyllabic sullenness:

> 'Have I not preved thus simply,
> Withoute any subtilite
> Of speche, or gret prolixite
> Of termes of philosophie,
> Of figures of poetrie,
> Or colours of rethorike?
> Pardee, hit oughte the to like!
> For hard langage and hard matere
> Is encombrous for to here
> Attones; wost hou not wel this?'
> And I answered and seyde, 'Yis.'
> 'A ha!' quod he, 'lo, so I can
> Lewedly to a lewed man
> Speke,[1] and shewe him swyche skiles[2]
> That he may shake hem be the biles,
> So palpable they shulden be.'

The eagle remains a bird even at his most schoolmasterly, and thinks of even arguments as having beaks. This deflating comedy is also found in book III, where the goddess Fame bellows at her suppliants like a fishwife:

---

[1] 'speak simply to an uneducated man'.   [2] 'such arguments'.

> 'Fy on yow', quod she, 'everychon!
> Ye masty swyn, ye idel wrechches,
> Ful of roten, slowe techches!
> What? false theves! wher ye wolde
> Be famous good, and nothing nolde
> Deserve why, ne never ye roughte?[1]
> Men rather yow to hangen oughte!'

None of this, however, can be said to integrate the poem, and along with its craziness of construction goes an uncertainty of tone which seems to reflect an uncertainty of intention. Some, indeed, have found it possible to read it as a parody of more solemn vision poems, such as *The Divine Comedy* itself; but it seems to veer uncontrollably between the comic and the serious. If it is difficult to imagine what the 'man of gret auctorite' could have said to bring the poem to a conclusive end, it is equally difficult to know how seriously Chaucer intends us to take him. Perhaps he himself did not know. He left works unfinished more often than we sometimes remember. From about the same period as *The House of Fame*, and sharing with it an oddly inflated rhetorical apparatus, is *Anelida and Arcite*, and there are also *The Legend of Good Women*, *The Canterbury Tales* as a whole, and a number of the separate tales within it. In persistently thinking of Chaucer as a classic, we have partly petrified his achievement; throughout his career he was an experimental writer, and there seems even to be something fragmentary, something centrifugal, in his whole outlook. In *The House of Fame*, at least, he produced an incomparably vivid and energetic fantasy, imagined with a sharpness that may be exemplified in the exact simile the Dreamer chooses to describe the murmur of voices in the House:

> 'And what soun is it lyk?' quod hee.
> 'Peter! lyk betinge of the see',
> Quod I, 'ayen the roches holowe,
> Whan tempest doth the shippes swalowe;
> And lat a man stonde, out of doute,
> A mile thens, and here hit route.'

---

[1] 'Would you achieve good fame, and yet are unwilling to do anything to deserve it, or even care about the matter?'

But if this imaginative realism was intended to serve some larger purpose, the purpose does not emerge.

In his next work in the dream-allegory tradition, *The Parliament of Fowls*, Chaucer achieves a new and entirely convincing assurance of tone. The poem derives from an even wider range of sources, French, Latin and Italian, and combines them seamlessly into a Chaucerian whole, couched in an easily flowing, richly textured verse. The French octosyllabic couplets of his earlier long poems have now been replaced by the decasyllabic stanzas of rime royal: more slowly moving, graver (though capable of including colloquialism without abruptness), and tending sometimes towards a processional effect, with each stanza presenting a separate scene or idea. The poem follows with an exactness that seems deliberate the pattern established in *The Book of the Duchess*: the reading of a book about a dream, followed by an actual dream influenced by the book, the dream being divided into two distinct episodes, a preliminary and then the main subject. The main subject is here the imagined meeting of the birds on St Valentine's day to choose their mates, and the poem was presumably written to accompany the St Valentine celebrations at Richard II's court. The apparent spontaneity, the dream-like unpredictability, of *The Book of the Duchess* has been lost as the pattern is repeated, and the dramatic projection of the Dreamer as a bewildered inhabitant of his own dream has been lost too—he is now, once he starts dreaming, little more than a neutral observer. In their place one finds a new richness of description, and description not merely of a decorative kind, but embodying moral discriminations so fully that they do not need to be stated.

The narrator is presented meditating on the perennial topic of love, and seeking in a book for an unstated 'certeyn thing'. The book is Cicero's *Somnium Scipionis*, a work which, with Macrobius' commentary on it, was a major influence on medieval dream-poetry. It tells how the younger Scipio Africanus was visited in a dream by the elder Africanus, who showed him the heavens and the destinations of human souls after death. The narrator then himself dreams of the elder Africanus, who leads him to the gate of a walled park, over which a double message is written:

> 'Thorgh me men gon into that blisful place
> Of hertes hele and dedly woundes cure;
> Thorgh me men gon unto the welle of grace,
> There grene and lusty May shal evere endure.
> This is the wey to al good aventure.
> Be glad, thow redere, and thy sorwe ofcaste;
> Al open am I—passe in, and sped thee faste!'
> 'Thorgh me men gon', than spak that other side,
> 'Unto the mortal strokes of the spere
> Of which Disdain and Daunger is the gyde,
> Ther nevere tre shal fruit ne leves bere.
> This strem yow ledeth to the sorweful were
> There as the fish in prisoun is al drye;
> Th'eschewing is only the remedye!'

The double inscription recalls that over the entrance to the other world in *The Divine Comedy*, but its reference has been changed, so that it now points to the two opposed aspects of secular love. With a touch of the old comedy, Africanus 'shoves' the Dreamer through the gate, and inside he finds a beautiful garden:

> A gardyn saw I ful of blosmy bowes
> Upon a river, in a grene mede,
> There as swetnesse everemore inow is,
> With floures white, blewe, yelwe, and rede,
> And colde welle-stremes, nothing dede,
> That swimmen ful of smale fishes lighte,
> With finnes rede and skales silver brighte.

It is a concentrated image of the rose-garden in the *Romaunt*, and of all the other gardens of love in medieval poetry, and it possesses in a sharpened form their ambivalence, as suggested by the inscriptions. It is surpassingly beautiful, paradisal even, yet its allegorical inhabitants, grouped around 'Cupide, oure lord', include such dubious characters as

> Foolhardinesse, Flaterye, and Desir,
> Messagerye, and Meede.

The Dreamer presses further into the garden, and comes upon a temple of brass, whose atmosphere is both exotic and sinister. It is full of lovers' sighs, which make the flames on the altars burn more fiercely, and in it the Dreamer finds first Priapus (the god of the sexual organs as well as of gardens) and then Venus herself. And Venus is presented as performing a kind of strip-tease act, which the Dreamer finds more provocative than mere nakedness: her breasts are naked, and her loins 'wel kevered to my pay' with semi-transparent drapery. Two young people are kneeling and praying for her help, and further in he sees painted the stories of women who died for love.

From this hothouse atmosphere the Dreamer re-emerges into the garden, where he sees the goddess Nature,

> . . . a queene,
> That, as of light the somer sonne shene
> Passeth the sterre, right so over mesure
> She fairer was than any creature.

She looks, Chaucer says, just as Alanus de Insulis described her in his *De Planctu Naturae*, a medieval Latin work directed against unnatural vices—another sign of Chaucer's wide reading. She is presiding over the annual meeting of the birds to choose their mates. Three noble male eagles (tercels) compete for the hand of a noble female eagle (formel), offering eminently courtly protestations of eternal devotion. The other species of birds join in, to offer advice, and also to protest against the length of these proceedings and their apparent remoteness from the motives of everyday life. Nature hears what they have to say, then silences them, and ordains that the formel shall be allowed to choose for herself which suitor she will accept. But the formel 'wol nat serve Venus ne Cupide' yet; she asks for a year's delay in making her choice, and this is granted. Nature assigns mates to all the other birds, they sing a roundel welcoming summer, and the noise of their song awakens the Dreamer, who is left reading still more books, in the hope of learning something that will benefit him.

The *Parliament* does not work round to any obvious conclusion in the form of a statement. Nevertheless, it conveys a very definite meaning in the form of two contrasts embodied in the actual dream-experience. The first of these contrasts is that between the realm of Venus and the realm of Nature: two aspects of sexual love, whose opposition is suggested by the double inscription over the gate. In the temple of Venus, enclosed, sultry, and somewhat sinister, with a perverse combination of exhibitionism and voyeurism at its centre, sexual love is presented as an enslaving obsession, barren and unproductive—

>   . . . the sorweful were
> There as the fish in prisoun is al drye.

Nature's realm, on the other hand, is one where order is combined with freedom. The birds are arranged hierarchically in their species, each has its spokesman, and Nature presides authoritatively over all; and yet there is real freedom of speech, and the formel is at liberty to choose or not to choose. The poem ends, as many medieval poems do, by offering its audience matter for further discussion—which suitor should she accept?—and this very inconclusiveness is the conclusive expression of the freedom possible under Nature's rule. The second contrast that the poem expresses is within Nature's realm itself, and forms part of this freedom. It is a contrast between courtly and non-courtly attitudes towards love. The three tercels are noble birds (indeed it has been suggested that they may stand for three actual courtiers of the day), and their attitudes towards love are refined and extreme: they are willing to fight to the death for their lady, or to die of love for her. But the other species of birds stand for lower social orders, and they express a vigorous contempt for such romantic notions. Their downright quacks and cackles resound in the verse—

> 'Ye quek!' yit seyde the doke, ful wel and faire,
> 'There been mo sterres, God wot, than a paire!'

The contrast between courtly romanticism and earthy 'realism' is found centrally elsewhere in Chaucer: for example, in the contrast between Troilus's and Pandarus's views of Criseyde. Here it cannot be said that Chaucer comes down on one side or the other. He simply allows full expression to the noble (but impracticable) attitudes of one side and to the realistic (but vulgar) attitudes of the other. We are to continue the dialogue in our own minds.

Chaucer's last employment of the dream-allegory form is also his first attempt at the framed collection of stories, a form which he was to develop further in *The Canterbury Tales*. The poem is *The Legend of Good Women*. The dream is confined to the Prologue, and the Dreamer is once again the voracious reader of the *Parliament*. But he is characterized much more fully than there, and more fully even than in *The House of Fame*, as an unsuccessful lover and a simple fellow, incapable of understanding his dream and even of understanding his own poetry. He is a writer, indeed, but a mere imitator and follower of authority—a deliberate parody of Chaucer's real achievement as 'translator'. The opposition between experience and authority suggested here is one of Chaucer's constant themes, as one might expect of a writer who is so deeply committed both to the world around him and to recreating foreign literatures in English. No resolution is offered in the *Legend*: Chaucer retreats behind his narrator's simple mask. The Dreamer is drawn from his books only in May, to admire his favourite flower, the daisy. He goes home at night, and dreams that he is back in the meadows looking for daisies. He finds instead the God of Love, crowned with roses as in the *Romaunt*, and with him a queen who *is* a daisy, transfigured. She is clothed in green and crowned with a white pearl surrounded by flowers. The whole conception is that of the medieval courtly 'religion of love', with the God of Love standing in place of the Christian God, and the queen in place of the Blessed Virgin. They are followed by a train of ladies, who sing a ballade in praise of this queen: she is Alcestis, who gave her life to redeem her husband from death. It emerges that the God of Love is angry with the Dreamer for having interfered with people's 'devocioun' to him by his 'translacioun' of the *Romaunt* and of *Troilus and Criseyde*—both works which show the love of women in a bad light. Alcestis rebukes the God for behaving more like a tyrant than a true king, and defends Chaucer by suggesting that he is foolish and did not fully understand what he translated:

> He may translate a thing in no malice,
> But for he useth bokes for to make,
> And taketh non hed of what matere he take,
> Therfore he wrot the Rose and ek Crisseyde
> Of innocence, and niste what he seyde.

The paradoxical position of the narrator is particularly clear at this point: he is at once identical with the poet Chaucer and ironically dissociated from him. Alcestis goes on to point out that Chaucer has also written in praise of love, in the dream-poems we have been examining, and also in *The Knight's Tale* (he had already begun work that was later to be collected in *The Canterbury Tales*). The God accepts the rebuke, and Chaucer eagerly takes up Alcestis's idea that he may have misunderstood his sources:

> ...what so myn auctour mente,
> Algate, God wot, it was myn entente
> To forthere trouthe in love and it cherice.

In the *Troilus* the Chaucerian narrator does indeed sometimes write as if he fails to understand the obvious implications of his sources, or is unwilling to accept those implications. Alcestis now imposes on the Dreamer a penance for his sins against love: to write a collection of tales of good women, martyred for the sake of the God of Love. It is to be a distinctly secular book of martyrs; the first of Love's saints is Cleopatra. Chaucer's task was straightforward—perhaps too straightforward to interest him. It may really have been imposed on him by some noble patroness, possibly the Queen herself, for one of the excuses Alcestis makes on his behalf for having written the *Romaunt* and the *Troilus* is that perhaps

> ...him was boden make thilke tweye
> Of som persone, and durste it not withseye.

At any rate the task does not seem to have been sympathetic. Love is the great Chaucerian subject, and in his earlier dream-poems, and still more in the *Troilus*, he had developed towards love an ironic and complex approach. He had now to abandon this, and to write simply of feminine virtue in love-matters, and the result is a series of brief narratives, borrowed mostly from Ovid, that are competently written certainly, but little more. Occasionally the verse comes to life in a single line—'Al for the love of Cleopataras' (601) or 'Yit last the venym of so longe ago' (2241)—but on the whole it is flat and neutral. He abridges rather than expands his sources, and as the work progresses he expresses his weariness more and more frequently, in such remarks as

> What shulde I more telle hir compleyning?
> It is so long, it were an hevy thing.

It was possibly boredom that caused him to abandon the *Legend* in mid-sentence, after writing only nine of the nineteen tales proposed. *The Legend of Good Women* is Chaucer's first attempt at a collection of tales, and also his first work (and probably the first work in English) to be written in decasyllabic couplets, which he was to use again in many of the best *Canterbury Tales*. But his particular gifts would naturally lead him to make the collection express a *variety* of different attitudes towards life; and here, outside the brilliant and subtle Prologue, only one attitude was possible.

Chaucer had already achieved a far greater variety of attitude in dealing with love in *Troilus and Criseyde*, although that is not a collection but a single work—indeed, his longest complete work. The story is of a love-affair that ended in betrayal. Troilus is a son of King Priam of Troy, and while Troy is being besieged by the Greeks he falls in love with Criseyde, the daughter of Calchas, a soothsayer who had learned that the Greeks were destined to capture Troy, and who had therefore deserted to them. With the help of some complicated manoeuvring by Pandarus—Criseyde's uncle and Troilus's close friend—the two lovers are brought together in secret. They consummate their love, and live in perfect happiness until the Greeks and Trojans arrange an exchange of prisoners, by which Criseyde is to be returned to her father. Troilus tries to persuade her to elope with him, but she refuses, promising that she will find some way for them to be reunited. In fact she becomes the mistress of a Greek, Diomede; and Troilus, when he learns of this, rushes madly into battle in the hope of finding Diomede, and is slain. The poem ends with Troilus's spirit ascending to heaven and condemning the 'blinde lust' of earthly life, and with the narrator begging his audience to turn from earthly to heavenly love. This basically simple story is presented by Chaucer as historical truth. It was not true, of course, nor did it possess even the half-truth of Homer's Trojan legend. So far as we know, it was invented by Benoît de Sainte-Maure, a twelfth-century French poet, and Chaucer's main source (though he had read Benoît) was a later retelling of the story by Boccaccio, the *Filostrato*. But Chaucer and his audience did not make our own sharp distinction between fiction and history; for them, it was enough for a story to have 'authority' behind it. In any case, Chaucer *uses* the supposed historical nature of his story chiefly as a means of emphasizing its general human truth: it was what did happen, and therefore what might happen. It is true that in the Prologue to the second of the poem's five books the narrator first invokes the historical muse and then apologizes if anything in the course of the love-affair should seem strange to his audience, because out of date. But this clash between historical truth and human truth is only momentary; it is immediately resolved in a sense of human variety—the difference between people is stressed, not the difference between historical periods. We are kept aware, certainly, of the Trojan setting of the story, and the approaching end of the lovers' happiness is presented as parallel to the approaching fall of the city. We are reminded, too, that the actors in the story are pagans, unlike Chaucer's Christian audience. Here, though, there is no real clash, for the poem seems to suggest that secular love is itself a kind of paganism, which offers to the human beloved a worship properly due to God. In general Chaucer presents his story as thoroughly contemporary. His 'modernization' in some ways makes the poem more distant from us, by making it follow specifically medieval patterns of thought; in other ways, by capturing a general human reality, he brings it nearer to us.

The love-affair follows a medieval courtly course—the very course prescribed in the *Roman de la Rose*. Troilus begins by scorning the God of Love and the folly of his devotees—'O veray fooles, nice and blinde ye be!'—and in return is struck by one of the God's arrows, and falls in love with Criseyde. For him, she is perfection itself; he does not know whether she is a woman or a goddess. Henceforward, his part in the story is emotional and passive, and in this respect he is likely to be an unsympathetic character to modern taste. His love makes him pale and ill—'sexti time a day he loste his hewe'—and he lies lamenting in his room, incapable of acting for himself. He employs a go-between (Pandarus); this too happens in the *Roman*. Once he thinks he stands a chance of acceptance, his love improves his character miraculously:

> For he bicom the frendlieste wight,
> The gentilest, and ek the mooste fre,
> The thriftiest and oon the beste knight,
> That in his time was or mighte be.

Although Troilus is unmarried and Criseyde a widow, their relationship must remain as secret as it if were adulterous, and the possibility of marriage is never mentioned. Hence the extreme complication of the plot by which they are eventually brought together, and Criseyde's unwillingness to elope with Troilus when the exchange is about to part them. Troilus's passivity remains throughout; he has to be engineered into bed with Criseyde, swooning on the way; he accepts their parting (though with reluctance); and in the last book he continues to believe her true to him long after it appears obvious that she cannot intend to return. At every crisis, we notice, his thoughts turn not to action but to his own death. In all these ways Chaucer's story may seem to be imprisoned in a specifically medieval convention; and we may feel the same too about its philosophic content. After first seeing Criseyde, Troilus is incited to a meditation on the paradoxical nature of love; after he is eventually brought

into bed with her he sings a song in praise of love borrowed by
Chaucer from Boethius's *De Consolatione Philosophiae* (of which he
had composed his English translation a little earlier); and when
faced with the prospect of losing her he embarks on a long consideration of destiny and freewill, again borrowed from Boethius.

From all this, *Troilus and Criseyde* sounds like a poem which
belongs to the past only, and not directly to us; yet from its beginning there are already signs of other elements mixed with the courtly
convention and fertilizing it. When Troilus first sees Criseyde, at
service in a temple, she is described as beautiful but modest and
retiring (we have just been told that she is in some danger because of
her father's treachery). Yet there is one word in the description which
strikes a slightly jarring note:

> ...she stood ful lowe and stille allone,
> Byhinden other folk, in litel brede,[1]
> And neigh the dore, ay undre shames drede,
> Simple of atir and debonaire of chere,[2]
> With ful assured loking and manere.

Why *assured*? The contrast between her modesty and her self-
possession is piquant, and suggests some hidden complexity of
character. A little later, when Troilus, to conceal his love-sickness,
has had it put about that he has a fever, the narrator comments:

> But how it was, certeyn, kan I nat seye,
> If that his lady understood nat this,
> Or feynede hire she niste,[3] oon of the tweye;
> But wel I rede that, by no manere weye,
> Ne semed it as that she of him roughte,[4]
> Or of his peyne, or whatsoevere he thoughte.

We have been given no reason to suppose that Criseyde knows
anything of Troilus's love; so why whould it be necessary to wonder
whether she was only pretending to know the meaning of his sickness? The narrator's attempt to interpret the bare fact given in his
sources has gratuitously thrown doubt on his heroine's motives.
Immediately after this Troilus is found weeping by Pandarus; and

[1] 'space'.　　[2] 'meek of countenance'.　　[3] 'pretended not to know'.　　[4] 'cared'.

in Pandarus, though he plays the traditional courtly role of go-
between, the tradition is not merely reproduced but modified.
Finding Troilus in solitary despair, he at once tries to make him
angry, 'And with an angre don his wo to falle'. He succeeds; and he
persuades Troilus to tell him the cause of his misery, speaking with a
briskness that strikes fire from Troilus himself:

> 'How hastow thus unkindely and longe
> Hid this fro me, thow fol?' quod Pandarus.
> 'Paraunter[1] thow mighte after swich oon longe
> That myn avis anoon may helpen us.'
> 'This were a wonder thing', quod Troilus.
> 'Thow koudest nevere in love thiselven wisse:[2]
> How devel maistow bringe me to blisse?'

The colloquial language of this exchange—an idiom still current in
the twentieth century—touches the courtly convention with human
realism. Throughout, this is the function of Pandarus, with his
energy, gaiety, and plausible speech. He tells Troilus:

> ...this nis naught, certein, the nexte wise
> To winnen love, as techen us the wise,
> To walwe and wepe as Niobe the queene,
> Whos teres yet in marble ben yseene,

and the exaggerated image has two effects. It makes us see Troilus's
grief in a more critical light, and it forces Troilus himself to define
the element of wilfulness in that grief:

> Nor other cure kanstow non for me.
> Ek I nil nat ben cured; I wol deye.
> What knowe I of the queene Niobe?
> Lat be thine olde ensaumples, I the preye.

Pandarus also promises to help his friend whoever the object of his
love may be:

> I kepe nat restreyne
> The[3] fro thi love, theigh that it were Eleyne
> That is thi brother wif, if ich it wiste:
> Be what she be, and love hire as the liste!

---

[1] 'perhaps'.   [2] 'guide'.   [3] 'I do not intend to keep you'.

137

Here, underlying Pandarus's practical good sense and hearty good fellowship, there is momentarily revealed a 'realism' of a different kind, a moral realism which involves a total lack of moral scruple. All the strands that have been mentioned as appearing in book I are interwoven throughout the poem: a courtly idealization that shades into absurdity; a convincing human realism; a moral 'realism' which shades into total amorality; and a doubtfulness about Criseyde—suspended between Troilus's idealization and Pandarus's realism—which is made the more suspicious by the uncertainties of the naïve historian-narrator.

We cannot follow out this interweaving of attitudes in detail, but it is worth looking at one or two points in the poem where it is particularly effective. One of these is the first consummation of love in book III. Here first Pandarus, even while acknowledging that he is virtually acting as a procurer for Troilus, begs him not to betray the victim any further by making their relationship public. In reply, Troilus denies that Pandarus's part is that of a bawd, because he is acting for friendship, not money, and then immediately discloses the true unscrupulousness of his behaviour by offering to do the same for Pandarus, even if the victim were his own sister! We seem to be embarked on an exposure of the ethics of the game of love, but in fact what follows shows the other side of the coin. Pandarus brings the lovers together in bed by a plot whose mechanics effectively reduce the dignity of love—he runs for a cushion for Troilus to kneel on to make his plea to Criseyde, then withdraws to read 'an old romaunce', only to rush back again when Troilus faints, in order to pull off his clothes and push him into bed with her. But now he retires again, taking away the candle with the dry remark that 'Light is nought good for sike folkes yen', and in Pandarus's absence Chaucer develops the scene of love-making with a superb and quite uncynical lyricism. There is probably no finer poetry of fulfilled love in English than this scene. Reality is never left behind: these are human lovers, and the attraction between them is richly physical, and is conveyed through images drawn from the natural world—the honeysuckle twisting round the tree, the nightingale frightened by the shepherd, and (far from sentimental) the lark seized by the sparrowhawk. But Chaucer also employs a train of religious imagery to convey the transcendent nature of their experience of love. Criseyde is Troilus's heaven, and in her he enjoys blessedness. The narrator is swept away with the lovers, drawn into their ecstasy:

> O blisful night, of hem so longe isought,
> How blithe unto hem bothe two thow weere!
> Why nad I swich oon with my soule ybought,
> Ye, or the leeste joie that was theere?

And yet even here some reservation is suggested, for perhaps this delightful service of Cupid *can* be bought only at the cost of one's soul.

From this triumph of love in book III we may turn to the poem's gloomy conclusion. The lovers are separated by the exchange of prisoners, and there can be no doubt that Criseyde's grief when she learns of this is genuine. It is expressed through a realism such as a novelist might use, in the description of the 'purpre ring' round her eyes, and in a brilliantly observed little scene in which her friends come bustling to congratulate her on her return to the Greeks but

> Although the body sat among hem there,
> Hire advertence is alwey elleswhere.

And yet Criseyde will not risk elopement with Troilus, and in the course of book V it gradually becomes clearer that she is never going to keep her promise to return. The previous dubiety surrounding her motives is now sharpened to a direct contradiction between two opposing views of her. Troilus, against all the evidence, persists in believing her faithful; Pandarus from the very beginning does not expect her to come back, and comments on Troilus's hopes with a caustic 'Ye, haselwode!'. The contradiction is seen at its sharpest when both are on the walls of Troy looking towards the Greek camp. They both see something moving; Troilus thinks it is Criseyde returning, Pandarus thinks it is only a wagon. Pandarus is right and Troilus wrong, but one cannot help finding in Troilus's deluded idealization a nobility of which Pandarus is incapable. Now Troilus's persistent tendency towards grief and thoughts of death has a suitable object, and is expressed in magnificent rhetoric, directed particularly at Criseyde's deserted house:

> Than seide he thus, 'O paleys desolat,
> O hous of houses whilom best ihight,
> O paleys empty and disconsolat,
> O thow lanterne of which queynt[1] is the light,
> O paleys, whilom day, that now art night,
> Wel oughtestow to falle, and I to dye,
> Syn she is went that wont was us to gye!'[2]

His idealizing love has now no object. The service of Cupid which he has followed previously has been exposed by Diomede's cruder following of the same pattern in *his* wooing of Criseyde:

> And wondreth nought, myn owen lady bright,
> Though that I speke of love to yow thus blyve;[3]
> For I have herd er this of many a wight,
> Hath loved thing he nevere saigh his live.
> Ek I am nat of power for to strive
> Ayeyns the god of Love, but him obeye
> I wole alwey; and mercy I yow preye.

Troilus is finally convinced of Criseyde's infidelity when he sees, pinned to a captured piece of Diomede's armour, a token which he himself had given to Criseyde. At the end of the poem the love of the Christian god is offered by the Christian narrator as a substitute for earthly love. There has been some controversy as to whether this conclusion is a mere afterthought, or whether it is the 'message' of the whole work. Perhaps neither of these extreme views is true: the conclusion 'feels right', but it can hardly be seen as the expression of an attitude consistently held by the narrator throughout. *Troilus and Criseyde* does not offer the overall consistency of attitude that one might expect from a modern novel. To see why this should be, we must finally look at the conditions of its publication.

Troilus and Criseyde was written for oral delivery to a courtly

[1] 'quenched'.   [2] 'Since she who used to guide us has departed'.   [3] 'quickly'.

audience. In one manuscript of the poem there is a picture showing Chaucer himself reading it aloud to the court of Richard II, and something like that must have been the circumstances of its original publication. The original audience would not have possessed copies of the poem, and one result of this, with a work so long that it would probably have had to be recited in instalments, is that it is constructed scene by scene. Each scene has its own unity, but *between* the scenes there are shifts in focus which are sometimes baffling when one tries to judge the work as a whole. A second result is that the poem presumes an intimate relationship between its narrator and its audience. The listeners are in the same room with him, they share his interests, and he can appeal directly to their own judgement of the story he tells. The role of this narrator is to mediate between the audience and an objective story which he takes from historical authorities. As usual, he is not simply the poet. He is as unsuccessful in love as his own Pandarus, yet he feels impelled to interpret the bare facts of his story for the listeners. His sources often leave him in ignorance, and he plaintively tells the listeners so; for example, when Pandarus, as part of his scheme to bring the lovers together, assures Criseyde that Troilus is not staying with him:

> Nought list myn auctour fully to declare
> What that she thoughte whan he seyde so,
> That Troilus was out of towne yfare,
> As if he seyde therof soth or no;
> But that, withowten await, with him to go,
> She graunted him, sith he hire that bisoughte,
> And, as his nece, obeyed as hire oughte.

He wishes to see the best in Criseyde—hence his superfluous 'as hire oughte'—but her unalterable role in the story sometimes makes this difficult. In such cases he may withdraw from judgement altogether: thus he says that 'the stories' say that Criseyde wept when Diomede was wounded by Troilus, and eventually 'Men seyn—I not—that she yaf him hire herte'. These uncertainties of the narrator most often refer to Criseyde—he does not even know how old she was, or whether she had any children—and their effect is generally to elicit from us a judgement severer than he himself makes, and than we should perhaps make if he would only hold his tongue. But it would be wrong to see the poem, as the God of Love saw it in the *Legend*, simply as a disguised attack on Criseyde and on the love of women. We are genuinely left to make up our own minds, by being given both the materials for judgement and the incitement to judge. The relationship between naïve narrator and experienced audience has the effect of suspending the story in an atmosphere rich with moral discrimination: we are drawn into the process of judgement, but the verdict is left to us.

Chaucer's combination in the *Troilus* of fixed, convincingly realized events with a variety of perspectives is taken to its culmination in his last major work, *The Canterbury Tales*. Here we find not a single narrator but a large number of narrators, brought together only as pilgrims to the shrine of St Thomas at Canterbury; and not a single tale but a large number of different tales, each capable of standing by itself as an independent work. The framed collection of stories was a common medieval literary form, at which, as we have seen, Chaucer had already made one attempt in *The Legend of Good Women*. There, however, the effect was one of monotony; now Chaucer went one better, and invented a literary form which would enable him to encompass the variety of his own view of life (and which, incidentally, would enable him to include a number of works he had already written). He chose perhaps the one story-telling occasion in medieval life which would bring together people of a wide range of classes, ages, occupations, and interests—a pilgrimage. In his *General Prologue* he introduces and describes some thirty people gathering together at the Tabard Inn in Southwark to go on a pilgrimage to Canterbury—a knight, a squire, a landowner, a rich merchant, a sailor, a doctor, a lawyer, a ploughman, tradesmen of all kinds, and people from various grades of the medieval Church. To these are joined Chaucer himself—the transformed Chaucer that we have come to expect—and the host of the Tabard, Harry Bailly.

Harry proposes a way of passing time on the journey: each pilgrim shall tell the others two tales on the way to Canterbury and two on the way back, and he himself will act as organizer and judge. This scheme, if completed, would have produced an enormous structure of over a hundred tales. In fact, at his death, Chaucer had written only twenty-four, and these are not all linked together by the pilgrimage framework, but are divided into a number of fragments, some of several tales, some of only one, and even the order of these fragments is uncertain. The effect is still of immense variety—the more completely various, perhaps, through the accident of being incomplete, and thus of *suggesting* still further points of view that might have been expressed. Indeed, one might even wonder whether this tantalizing incompleteness really is accidental; for surely the impulse in Chaucer that led him to present life in terms of variety was the same that drove him in middle age to take up a scheme so vast that he was unlikely to bring it to a conclusion. It is clear, at least, that variety was what Chaucer was aiming at from the beginning. We have *The General Prologue* and the first four tales in a finished form. The first pilgrim to tell a tale is chosen by lot, and the lot falls appropriately on the Knight, the person of highest secular rank. He tells his tale—one of knightly deeds in love and war—and the Host invites the Monk to tell the next. But the Miller, who is drunk, insists that he will speak next, and the Host gives way. His tale is of a quite different kind, a comic story of bawdy ingenuity in a lower-class setting. Before it, Chaucer inserts a few sentences of his own:

> What sholde I moore seyn, but this Millere
> He nolde his wordes for no man forbere,
> But tolde his cherles tale in his manere.
> M'athynketh that I shal reherce it heere.[1]
> And therefore every gentil wight I preye,
> For Goddes love, demeth nat that I seye
> Of yvel entente, but for I moot reherce
> Hir tales alle, be they bettre or werse,
> Or elles falsen som of my mateere.

[1] 'I regret that I have to repeat it here'.

And therfore, whoso list it nat yheere,
Turne over the leef and chese another tale;
For he shal finde ynowe, grete and smale,
Of storial thing that toucheth gentillesse,
And eek moralitee and hoolinesse.
Blameth nat me if that ye chese amis.

Chaucer is here speaking as poet as well as pilgrim, and though we cannot take his apology literally (for it depends on our believing that the pilgrimage and its tales really happened), still it is clear that he is offering us variety and choice. He does not seem to imagine *The Canterbury Tales* simply as being read aloud to a small and homogeneous audience, in the same way as the *Troilus*, but also as being circulated in manuscript among people of different tastes.

In real life the variety of tellers would no doubt produce a variety of tales, but it would also produce variety of a more distinct kind according to the medieval literary theories that were examined in ch. 4. The *artes poeticae* present the literary styles and genres as being arranged in a hierarchy that corresponds to the hierarchical structure of medieval society. Thus a 'gentil' such as the Knight or the Squire, or one aspiring to be 'gentil' such as the Franklin, would naturally tell some 'storial thing that toucheth gentillesse', while an ecclesiastic or learned person such as the Monk, Prioress, Clerk, or Parson would tell of 'moralitee and hoolinesse'. These are the respectable medieval literary forms, stories told by literate people and usually having the authority of books behind them—the Knight's story, for example, is taken from Boccaccio, and the Clerk's from Petrarch. But correspondingly a 'cherl' such as the Miller or Reeve or Summoner will inevitably tell 'a cherles tale in his manere', and this fact enabled Chaucer to introduce into *The Canterbury Tales* a new kind of material. All his previous work, as we have seen, had been closely related to identifiable written sources, French, Latin, or Italian. But now he is able to include stories of a less dignified kind, sometimes taken from deliberately 'low' literary traditions, such as the French *fabliaux*, sometimes even passed from mouth to mouth without the intervention of writing. And these stories, though they may be polished and elaborated by Chaucer, still retain a superbly farcical coarseness, often expressed in the vigorous idiom of everyday speech. In these tales Chaucer's seemingly effortless realism reaches its height, and he pushes even further that 'solidity of specification' which he had developed in *Troilus and Criseyde* and which Henry James calls the supreme virtue of fiction. In *The Miller's Tale*, for example, by small repeated touches he gradually builds up a fully detailed picture of the carpenter's house—the red cover on the cupboard in the student's room, the hole that the cat used to creep through, and the chest-high hinged window. Again, in *The Summoner's Tale* the begging friar's whole nature is caught exactly in the gesture with which he brushes away the cat before sitting down and in his whining speech, with its repeated button-holing 'Thomas, Thomas'. And this very solidity may reach out towards myth or symbol, as in the country images—weasel, swallow, kid, stored apples—used to describe the carpenter's wife Alisoun.

The correspondence between social type and literary type is one of the bases of *The Canterbury Tales*. Beyond this, though a few of the tales seem to have no reason for belonging to one pilgrim rather than another, most of them have a particular appropriateness to their actual tellers. For example, the Knight and his son, the Squire, are both 'gentils'. They are presented in *The General Prologue* as typical figures rather than as unique individuals like the Wife of Bath or the Pardoner—the Knight elderly, somewhat old-fashioned, a veteran of many wars against the heathen, devoted to the traditional knightly ideals of 'Trouthe and honour, fredom and curteisie', the Squire young, dressed gaily in the height of fashion, full of courtly accomplishments, and an ardent lover. Both offer in their tales 'storial thing that toucheth gentillesse'—examples of chivalric romance, in which the setting is aristocratic and idealized, the characters are great figures from history or legend, and their actions are noble and concern love and war. But despite this identity of genre, the two tales have a very different effect, and the difference is related to their tellers. *The Knight's Tale* takes to its fullest development the image of human life implicit in romance—life seen as pageant or ritual, in which every action has a meditated symmetry and nobility. The tale concerns the competition between two scarcely distinguishable knights for the hand of a lady, and in it even conflict to the death takes the aesthetically pleasing form of a tournament. Yet, precisely by being attributed to the Knight, the fine simplicity of this view of life is tested against actual experience and offered as a matter for our own judgement. In describing the great flocking of chivalry towards the tournament arranged by the lady's brother-in-law to settle the dispute, the Knight pauses to add

> For if ther fille tomorwe swich a cas,
> Ye knowen wel that every lusty knight
> That loveth paramours and hath his might,
> Were it in Engelond or elleswhere,
> They wolde, hir thankes, wilnen to be there—
> To fighte for a lady, *benedicitee!*
> It were a lusty sighte for to see.

We respect the enthusiastic idealism which can see this chivalric behaviour in a contemporary setting, but we are also driven to recognize the actual remoteness of the Knight's imaginative world from Chaucer's England. It is remote at least so far as its idealism is concerned; but even within that imaginative world itself—the world of beautiful ladies in beautiful gardens, of extravagant courage and devotion—there are signs of conflict. For the story tells of destruction, of pain and misery brought upon human beings by gods concerned only with their own dignities. It concludes with a long philosophical speech by Theseus, the lady's brother, in which he attempts to fit this destructive element into a pattern of divine order; and this speech is a magnificent embodiment of intellectual struggle, of the *difficulty* philosophy has in accounting for certain aspects of human life. These modifications of the basic romance vision turn *The Knight's Tale* into a work which at once expresses and transcends the essential qualities of medieval romance. It is one of the supreme achievements of courtly literature in the Middle Ages. In *The Squire's Tale*, on the other hand, it is the limitations of romance of which we are made most conscious. The Squire's story (which is incomplete) is set exotically in the court of Genghis Khan in Tartary, and its action is far more extravagant than that of *The Knight's Tale*—it involves a flying horse of brass, a magic mirror, an invincible sword, a ring that enables its possessor to understand the language of birds, and other wonders. One marvel presses fast upon another, and the tale is pervaded by a breathless eagerness which clearly belongs to the young Squire himself—

> But hennesforth I wol my proces holde
> To speken of aventures and of batailles,
> That nevere yet was herd so grete mervailles!

Here romance, untouched by the deeper notes of *The Knight's Tale*, is put in its place as the product of youthful fantasy—the Franklin tells the Squire that he has spoken well, 'consideringe thy yowthe' —but utterly remote from the real world. A third variation on the romance theme occurs in the tale Chaucer gives to himself. The romance was originally an aristocratic continental genre. When it crossed the Channel to England, it tended to go down in the social scale, and to present a cruder version of aristocratic life, as seen from below. There exists a whole group of English 'tail-rhyme' romances, written in jerky stanzas, with short lines, their style clumsy and full of the minstrel's padding, and their subject-matter absurd or banal. Chaucer's *Tale of Sir Thopas* is brilliant parody of this debased form of romance. He could not have made the parody so complete and so devastating unless he had read a large number of tail-rhyme romances, and it is interesting to have this evidence of his reading in English. Much has been said about his study of French, Italian, and Latin, but what else he had read in his own language it is difficult to say. Certainly he knew of alliterative poetry, and the opening of *The Squire's Tale* has enough similarities to *Sir Gawain and the Green Knight* for some to believe that he had read that masterpiece of the Alliterative Revival. In *Sir Thopas*, however, he makes fun of one kind of English poetry, and in doing so takes the role of idiot-poet to its culmination. Chaucer the pilgrim tells the tale with the utmost seriousness and enthusiasm, quite oblivious of its absurdity:

> Sire Thopas wax a doghty swain;
> Whit was his face as payndemayn,[1]
>   His lippes rede as rose;
> His rode[2] is lyk scarlet in grain,
> And I yow telle in good cetrain,
>   He hadde a semely nose.

When the Host, unable to endure any more, rudely interrupts him—'Thy drasty[3] ryming is nat worth a toord!'—poor Chaucer is deeply hurt, and substitutes for it 'a litel thing in prose', which turns out to be the long and uninspired allegory of *Melibee and Prudence*. This is scarcely a joke; and in defence of *Melibee*, one must remember that Chaucer found room in *The Canterbury Tales* for an even longer prose piece by the Parson, which has equally little appeal to modern tastes, and which was clearly intended seriously.

We may take a briefer look at the individual variations played on another theme, that of 'moralitee and hoolinesse'. As we should expect, the Prioress, the Clerk and the Pardoner are all given material of this kind, but once again their individual tales have quite different effects, and effects which all undercut the simple surface meanings of their subject-matter. The Prioress tells a pathetic tale of a small boy who was murdered by Jews, but whose corpse, by a miracle of the Blessed Virgin, continued to sing the anthem 'Alma redemptoris mater' after his death, so that his murderers were brought to justice. But the Prioress has been presented in a quietly subversive way in *The General Prologue* as a lady more devoted to secular refinement than to spiritual virtue, and one whose 'conscience and tendre herte' are concentrated on her pet dogs rather than on her human neighbours. Thus the pathos of her tale is deliberately sentimentalized, particularly through a relentless repetition of certain emotion-producing words, such as 'mooder', 'child' and 'litel'—'This litel child, his

---

[1] 'fine bread'.   [2] 'complexion'.   [3] 'filthy'.

litel book lerninge'. The effect is of a self-indulgent pleasure in the emotions aroused by brutality juxtaposed with innocence. The Clerk's story is of a lord who marries a poor peasant girl, and then subjects her, over twenty years, to the most appalling tests of her submission and patience, including taking away her children and pretending that he has had them murdered. At the end of all this, convinced of her perfection, he takes her back into his favour. The Clerk tells this story in such a way that we can see it now realistically, as a horrifying study in obsession on the husband's part—

> ...ther been folk of swich condicion
> That whan they have a certein purpos take,
> They kan nat stinte of hire entencion,
> But, right as they were bounden to a stake,
> They wol nat of that firste purpos slake

—and now allegorically, as a parable of God's testing of the human soul. Neither view of the story is established as the 'right' one, and the double perspective is at once disturbing and stimulating. Finally, in the Pardoner we have a man whose very way of life—selling God's pardon for his own profit—is a blasphemous form of cupidity. He is therefore given a tale of terrifying power about three blasphemers who set out to kill Death, and who in fact kill each other through their greed for money. In its very structure this tale is a blasphemous parody, for the death of Death is a central Christian idea.

For further comment on the individual tales the reader must turn to the introductions to the separate volumes in this series. This is the appropriate place, however, for a few remarks about the *relationships* between the tales. The pilgrims are thrust into a community. We do not simply hear the stories they tell, we also catch glimpses of their reactions to the stories told by the others, of their appreciation, agreement, disagreement, and, often enough, as we might expect of such a mixed bag of people, of their quarrels. These reactions are displayed in the link passages between the tales, which contain some of Chaucer's liveliest writing, and which also indicate the gradual movement of the pilgrimage towards Canterbury. The relationships between the pilgrims influence the tales they tell. At its most obvious level, we can see this in a case such as that of the Miller and the Reeve. *The Miller's Tale* is about an old carpenter, living near Oxford, who is married to a delectable young wife, and is ingeniously cuckolded by the student who lodges with them. The Reeve is a carpenter by trade, and he takes this story as a personal attack on himself. He therefore answers it by telling a tale of his own about a miller, living near the other university of Cambridge, who tries to cheat two students, and in return has his wife seduced by one and his daughter by the other. Similarly, there is no love lost between the Summoner and the Friar, and so the Friar tells a story about a villainous summoner who is carried off by a devil, and the Summoner one about a cunning friar who receives an unexpected reward. We can also find more complex relationships among several tales, which seem to form part of a debate among the pilgrims on the subject of marriage, and more particularly on the question of 'sovereinetee' (mastery) in marriage. (Here, though, we must tread carefully, because the tales concerned belong to several fragments, and it is not sure in what order Chaucer would eventually have placed them.) The Wife of Bath first embarks on an autobiographical prologue, in which she vigorously expounds her belief in marriage rather than virginity, and in female dominance—*her* dominance—in marriage, and recalls her relations with the five husbands she has run through so far. This Prologue, for all its apparent individuality and spontaneity—

> But now, sire, lat me se, what shal I seyn?
> A ha! by God, I have my tale ageyn

—is modelled on a long speech in Jean de Meun's part of the *Roman de la Rose*, and also draws on much learned writing in Latin for its discussion of marriage. She then tells a story which not only acts as an *exemplum* supporting her arguments, but is also a perfect example of wish-fulfilment. It concerns a young knight who was condemned to death for rape (and would therefore be virile enough to make the Wife an ideal husband). He has imposed on him, to save his life, the task of discovering the thing that women most desire. An ugly old hag tells him the right answer—'sovereinetee'—but in return demands that he should marry her. He does so, but her ugliness and low birth make him reluctant to consummate the marriage; whereupon, once he has promised to accept *her* 'sovereinetee', she promptly transforms herself by magic into a young and beautiful lady. What more could the Wife wish for herself? The Clerk's Tale of the cruelly dominant husband and submissive wife acts as an answer to this story; at the end of it he ironically advises wives to follow the example of the Wife of Bath, and not that of the patient wife in his story. The Merchant, an old man newly married to a young wife, tells a tale reflecting his own situation, and directed against marriage itself. It is a brilliant study in self-deception, in which another newly married old man, whose physical appearance is described with a horrifyingly cold realism—'The slakke skin aboute his nekke shaketh'—suffers the usual fate of being cuckolded. The Franklin, on the other hand, tells a tale about a married couple who seem to have solved the problem of 'sovereinetee' by combining the male dominance of medieval marriage with the female dominance of medieval courtship, so that both are master and both servant. But this solution raises further problems, and though the potentially tragic tale has a happy ending, it remains problematic. A mocking echo of the marriage discussion may be heard in *The Nun's Priest's Tale*, a beast-fable in which cock and hen stand for man and wife, and the cock nearly comes to a sad end by succumbing to the charms of his favourite wife and disregarding an ominous dream.

There exists, then, a certain thematic coherence embracing a number of tales in which marriage is a central issue. Coherence, though, may take the form of contrast or parody as well as debate, and this is also an important link between certain tales. *The Knight's Tale*, for example, is immediately followed by *The Miller's Tale*, explicitly offered by its teller to 'quite' (answer) its predecessor. In *The Knight's Tale* a courtly dilemma is established between two knights and one lady, with whom both are in love. In *The Miller's*

Tale the same triangle reappears, but now the actors are a student, a parish clerk, and a luscious young 'wenche'. The fine language of 'curteisye' and 'mercy' is still used, but it is now not the expression of nobility of nature, but the barest of disguises for straightforward animal desire. An even more striking relationship of a similar kind exists between *The Monk's Tale* and *The Nun's Priest's Tale*. The Monk tells not one story but a whole series of 'tragedies', dismal tales of the fall of the great into misery, beginning with Lucifer and Adam, and threatening to continue for ever. He is interrupted politely by the Knight and less politely by the Host, who both demand something more cheerful. This the Monk refuses to provide, and so the Nun's Priest takes his place. Now the Monk's last 'tragedie' had been the story of Croesus, which involves an ominous dream and its fulfilment. The Nun's Priest tells a mock-'tragedie', also showing how a bad dream came true, in which the main characters are a cock, a hen, and a fox. The mockery in his story is directed not simply against his animal-characters, but against the *human* aspiration embodied in them and in the Monk's heroes—the pretension to be creatures of tragic destiny, a pretension expressed particularly in the rhetorical 'high style' of 'Gaufred'. The juxtaposition with *The Monk's Tale* is an essential part of this effect.

We have found in *The Canterbury Tales* both a linking of tales to tellers and significant relationships of different kinds among the tales themselves. But the essence of the work's total effect remains variety, and variety not of a fortuitous kind, but the expression of a distinctive attitude towards life. Chaucer is famous as the great poet of human reality, the one writer of so long ago in whose characters we can recognize our own neighbours. If he is the poet of reality, it is because he is not the poet of any single view of reality. He forces us to acknowledge that a whole range of views is possible and necessary, and he always calls our own judgements into play. This is the Chaucer whose development I have tried to make clear in this chapter.

6. CHAUCER'S SCIENCE

Our first, and perhaps our strongest impression of Chaucer is likely to be of a deeply knowing observer of the comedy of human affairs, and an unerring judge of character. We may feel inclined to say of him what Dryden claimed for Shakespeare, that he was naturally learned, and 'needed not the spectacles of books to read nature'. No one who had read much of *Troilus and Criseyde* or of *The Canterbury Tales* could deny Chaucer's amused and tolerant understanding, both of men and of women, or the judgement that comes from human experience outside the limits of formal education. At the same time, no attentive reader could overlook the signs of Chaucer's learning. *The General Prologue* alone reveals a familiar acquaintance with many professional subjects, as well as with all types of men. Chaucer refers to the Clerk's course of university studies, to the writings of St Augustine, to the Physician's expertise as an astrologer, and to the Man of Law's drafting of conveyances, with the assurance of a man possessing a wide knowledge of intellectual matters. The formidable list of medical authorities studied by the Physician suggests that Chaucer's interest in this pilgrim's intellectual background was as keen as his observation of the man's dress and habits. Chaucer's picture of himself as a studious recluse, dazing himself by reading books far into the night, cannot be a complete travesty of fact. His poetry reveals a lively intelligence, working in harmony with a great imaginative gift, and maintaining an active interest in the philosophical and scientific beliefs of his age.

This interest is displayed most convincingly in two prose works, the translation of Boethius, entitled *Boece*, and the *Treatise on the Astrolabe*, an instrument used in making astrological calculations. The philosophy of Boethius, relating to fortune and predestination, found its way into *The Knight's Tale* and into *Troilus and Criseyde*, and seems to have influenced Chaucer's outlook appreciably. But his intellectual interests were not confined to a few authors and topics. Although the problems of predestination, the study of astrology and the nature of dreams may have held some special fascination for Chaucer, his mind ranges widely through the sphere of human knowledge. The Nun's Priest mentions a Latin authority on mermaids, the Wife of Bath quotes Seneca, Dante and St Jerome, and in his Tale the Squire refers to a great Arabian authority on optics. With others, these characteristically varied allusions indicate a breadth of reading and of scientific interests such as a few modern writers might possess. When we take into consideration the difficulty of obtaining books before printing had been introduced, the extent of Chaucer's learning seems even more remarkable. We recognize that he is the poet not merely of medieval English society, but of the intellectual life of the time.

We should not study medieval science simply to understand allusions to the four humours or the planetary influences, but to make some acquaintance with the intellectual climate in which Chaucer lived. Without some knowledge of medieval astronomy, the comment that

> the yonge sonne
> Hath in the Ram his halve cours yronne,

will be lost on us, though the lively pulse of the line and the sense of energy compressed into the animal image must convey some of its meaning. What we shall not appreciate is the mental habit of referring to the annual movement of the heavens rather than to the calendar to determine the date of an occurrence; not because calendars were unknown to Chaucer, but because an astrological fix represents appreciably more than a bare date. Beside indicating the progress of the year, it gives the day a specific character by placing it within the context of heavenly influences which affect all life on earth. Thus, in addition to indicating the time of year and the emotional temper of the season, Chaucer's reference shows his mental habit of associating even minor features of human life with some greater system, binding together aspects of existence which we consider unrelated. Most of the basic beliefs of medieval science and philosophy rested upon an assumption that the world had been created to a logically ordered design, and that all its individual objects and creatures shared some community of purpose or constitution which drew them together. The modern habit of examining things in isolation, of inquiring into their particular nature rather than of trying to discover their function in a grand universal design, would have been completely alien to Chaucer. A knowledge of the kind of belief which medieval science encouraged enables us to sense the intellectual atmosphere which surrounded Chaucer and helped to shape his habit of thought.

Medieval science was for the greater part second-hand and derivative. It did not spring from original research and discovery, but was firmly based upon the philosophy of the ancient world which Arabian scholars revived and disseminated into western Europe during the twelfth century. Unlike modern scientific theories, its principles were not exposed to re-appraisal of any radical kind, and the authority of its leading figures remained undisputed until the rise of empirical science five centuries later. The most formidable resistance to the re-establishment of scientific learning in the Middle Ages came from the Church, which at first saw the veneration of Aristotle as a challenge to the authority of its own doctrines. The revealed truth of religion and the scientific truth which man reached through the use of reason were found to conflict. Aristotle had based his approach to problems of natural science on the assumption that everything existed for the end which it served, and that through reason man could discover the essential nature of things. The Church preferred to believe that man could become aware of the divine purpose only through revelation, expressed in Scripture or the writings of the Fathers. This conflict between theology and Aristotelian philosophy was reconciled by Aquinas, a thirteenth-century scholar and divine, who argued that two distinct points of view were involved, and that each was effective within its own sphere of inquiry. Through the summaries of Aquinas the scientific thought of the ancient world was presented to the Middle Ages as a codified system of belief, and accommodated to the outlook of the medieval Church. The fact that the ancient philosophers had been pagans could not be held to discredit their work. Medieval Europe had no comparable talent for scientific inquiry, and no means of replacing Aristotelian physics or Ptolemaic geography by systems of its own devising. The medieval Church was obliged to come to terms with pre-Christian thought by harmonizing its own doctrines and those of the ancient scientists. Thus Aquinas argued that Aristotle's belief that the universe was eternal could be neither proved nor disproved by reason, and must therefore be denied on the authority of revealed truth.

This fusion of beliefs produced Scholasticism, in which scientific inquiry was assigned a role immediately subordinate to the study of divinity, by which man could hope to fathom God's purposes. With the double authority, Scholasticism was strongly armed against every form of intellectual challenge, but few medieval minds were disposed to question the basic assumptions of contemporary science. The world had been created by a God who had ordained a particular function for every creature and object. The task of the natural philosopher was to discover this function, and so eventually to understand, however dimly, the organization of the great interlocking system of life which God had brought into being. The predominant interests of medieval science were not empirical but philosophical and speculative, and its inquiries were bound up with the central problem of man's existence and divine purpose. The impulse of modern science to extend the boundaries of knowledge by asking new questions, or by re-examining accepted conclusions, was foreign to the temper of medieval thought.

But medieval science was not completely inert. The popular notion that medieval scholars wasted their energies in fruitless inquiries about the substantiality of angels does injustice to the serious work of men like Bradwardine and Buridan in the field of physics. Their attempts to explain the nature of movement and velocity contributed something to the better understanding of these phenomena, and might have interested others who were not primarily scientists. Again, some attempts to verify Aristotelian principles experimentally were made by Grosseteste and Roger Bacon at Oxford during the thirteenth century, and by a number of continental scientists of whom Albertus Magnus was the most famous. At Bologna and other cities of northern Italy the study of human anatomy was advanced by Mondino and others, who dissected both male and female bodies. It would be wrong, therefore, to represent medieval science as completely lacking the spirit of original inquiry. In general, however, and especially during the later Middle Ages, it failed to move towards the solution of the practical scientific problems which confronted the age, or to establish a new basis of scientific thought. 'From the beginning of the fourteenth century to the end of the sixteenth', a modern historian of science observes,

there was a tendency for the best minds to become increasingly interested in problems of pure logic divorced from experimental practice, just as in another field they became more interested in making purely theoretical, though also necessary, criticisms of Aristotle's physics without bothering to make observations.[1]

Throughout the period of Chaucer's life, scientific thought lacked any appreciable impetus. The activities of fourteenth-century scientists were confined to the reaffirmation of old ideas, and to amplifying theories whose truth had never been demonstrated.

Medieval science was, however, a province of thought filled with colourful and humanly attractive beliefs, which an intelligent layman could follow without first mastering higher mathematics or principles remote from everyday experience. An omnivorous reader, Chaucer clearly interested himself in the scientific outlook of his age, making it part of his imaginative life and allowing it to affect his consciousness of the world about him. There is nothing poetically

[1] A. C. Crombie, *Augustine to Galileo* (1959), II, 22.

incongruous about the scientific investigations which he carries out during his celestial flight in *The House of Fame*, when the Eagle invites him to inspect the 'ayerissh creatures' of cloud, mist, rain and wind, spoken of by Plato. Besides intellectual enlightenment, science has brought the poet a great field of imaginative experience which he explores with astonishment and delight. The Eagle's long scientific discourse on the nature of movement fits appropriately into the flight which shows Chaucer the whole expanse of the earth, with towns and rivers, and the shapes of beasts in the forests, as part of man's universal environment. Following Aristotle's theory of dynamics, the Eagle argues

> That every kindely thing that is
> Hath a kindely stede ther he
> May best in hit conserved be;
> Unto which place every thing
> Thorgh his kindely enclining,
> Moveth for to come to,
> Whan that hit is awey therfro.[1]

Supported by this scientific premise, he declares that sound—which is 'noght but eyr ybroken'—rises from its point of origin in the same way that ripples extend in widening circles across the surface of water. By this means everything spoken on earth finds its way to the House of Fame. The Eagle's theory is of course merely fanciful, but the analogy is drawn in a manner which makes the idea seem inherently probable. Chaucer is turning contemporary scientific belief to his own advantage as poet, and showing through the Eagle an affectionate familiarity with the ideas and methods of medieval science. So far from regarding scientific inquiry as an activity alien to the work of the poet, Chaucer associates the two; finding in the hypotheses of the one the imaginative material of the other.

---

[1] *The House of Fame*, 730–6. 'Every natural object or creature has a natural place where it is at rest and not subject to change, and towards which it is prompted to move whenever it is elsewhere.' The Eagle's assertion that this doctrine is in every philosopher's mouth, 'as Aristotle and daun Platon', is a Chaucerian joke. Plato held a rather different opinion.

The medieval view of cosmic order characterized the appealing simplicity of contemporary scientific outlook, and its concern to establish the regularity of the system which natural laws seemed designed to maintain. The earth stood fixed at the centre of the universe, surrounded by the seven stars or planets which revolved about it as satellites, each in its own sphere, like a series of concentric glass balls placed one inside the other. The sphere of the moon—the first of these so-called planets—divided the universe into two distinct regions, terrestrial and celestial. Beneath the moon, all bodies were subject to the four kinds of change defined by Aristotle: motion, alteration of size and of quality, and change of substance through the process of generation or of decay. Above the sphere of the moon, bodies were composed of an incorruptible element or quintessence, and were subject only to change of position. Beyond the sphere of the outermost planet, Saturn, lay the zone of the fixed stars and the Primum Mobile, by which the hand of God imparted movement to the whole system of the universe. The earth itself comprised four zones, of which the highest—the zone of fire—lay above the atmosphere. Below the air lay the zones of water and earth, the lowest of the four. From these essential substances, or elements, all matter had been created, and from the elemental qualities of hot, cold, wet and dry, individual objects derived their particular character. We should think of the four elements not as material substances, but as invisible essences or spirits which imparted heat, weight, moistness and other attributes to things, depending upon the proportion of each element which the object contained. If it was hot and dry, this proved a preponderance of the fiery element; if cold and heavy, the element of earth predominanted. Such statements may seem to represent a form of rudimentary chemical analysis, but in fact—though the old philosophers did not realize this—they did no more than indicate the presence of qualities which everyone could observe. To say that the element of air predominated was no different from remarking that the object was felt to be light. What seemed a scientific statement was actually a description of physical attributes, and typical of the old philosophy in its concern with qualities which a human observer could feel or sense, rather than calculate.

Every object contained parts of all four elements, since without the complementary qualities of hot to modify cold, or of moist to relieve the dry, the complete predominance of one element would consume it. The practice of medieval medicine was largely directed towards preserving a healthy balance of elemental qualities within the patient's body. A man suffering from a burning fever was in danger of death because the qualities of moist and cold had become exhausted, and unable to repress the fiery spirit which gave the body its living heat. The task of the physician—who, of course, knew nothing of virus infection—was to restore the lost balance through treatment designed to renew the missing qualities, here of moist and cold. Chaucer's 'verray, parfit praktisour'

> knew the cause of everich maladye,
> Were it of hoot, or coold, or moiste, or drye,
> And where they engendred, and of what humour.

Within the human body the elemental qualities were derived from four humours or vital juices, each of them essential to life. The most obvious of them was blood, to which was given the warm, moist character corresponding to the element of air. The other three were choler, corresponding to fire; phlegm, and melancholy or black bile, which as heaviest of the four was made to correspond with earth. A man in whom the four humours were combined in exactly equal proportions, it was believed, would live forever; but in practice it was found that every person had a preponderance of one humour in his physiological make-up. This was not necessarily a possible source of illness, but rather a basis of individual character or temperament. If the humour of melancholy predominated, the temperament would be heavy and sombre; if choler, quick and irascible. An excess of phlegm produced a cold, sluggish character; and when the humour of blood predominated, it gave rise to a sanguine[1] temperament—bold, joyful and amorous. Thus the particular combination of humours within the body gave rise to four types of individuality or 'complexion', classified as sanguine, choleric, phlegmatic and melancholic; each determining psychology and personal appearance. Where the modern sense of 'complexion' applies only to the face, in Middle English the term covered individual temperament and also the shape and condition of the body. By remarking of the Franklin,

> Of his complexioun he was sangwyn,

Chaucer shows that he had a cheerful rosy face, and implies that he was healthy, vigorous and confident. The account of the Franklin's hospitality and sociableness follows naturally in a man of his complexion. The Host is identified as another sanguine character by his good humour, manly physique and love of company. On the other hand, the Miller's coarse appetite, quarrelsome temper and brutishness prove him choleric; excessive heat having twisted his nature violently out of shape. His red beard associates him with the Summoner, whose 'fyr-reed cherubinnes face', vulgarity and drunken rowdiness are marks of the same complexion, and with the Wife of Bath; intemperate, brazen and bent on conquest, a feminine counterpart of the thick-set Miller, who 'wolde have alwey the ram'. Most of the pilgrims fall into these two categories, perhaps because the energy of Chaucer's writing found a ready outlet through such full-blooded figures. The Clerk, withdrawn and starved of living substance, is probably phlegmatic in complexion, like the valetudinarian Physician who follows a careful diet 'of greet norissing and digestible'. Only two pilgrims, the Reeve and the Pardoner, seem to be classifiable as melancholic. Both have the touch of death in themselves, one aping liveliness despite the obvious signs of his sterility, the other freezing all cheerfulness and sociability by his deliberate malice. Chaucer begins by describing the Reeve as choleric, but comparison with the Miller and the Summoner shows

---

[1] From French *sanguin*, 'relating to blood'.

that in him the immoderate heat of choler has now exhausted itself, leaving a man parched and without warmth, his rage congealed into a hatred of all life.

Individual temperament was determined by a predominance of one of the humours. This predominance was in turn caused by planetary influences, acting upon man as upon every earthly creature and course of events. Whichever planet or sign happened to be strongest at the moment of a man's birth implanted its influences in his being, and continued to affect his constitution, for good or for evil, throughout his life. *The Knight's Tale* and *The Franklin's Tale* make it clear that the effects of such planetary influences were not limited to states of health, but played a decisive part in deciding his personal fortunes. Man was as continuously exposed to such forces as to the weather, or as the sea to the influence of the moon, which medieval science accounted one of the seven planets. Just as this planet could cause tides and promote natural growth, so the other heavenly bodies and signs stimulated or checked the progress of every being, plant or state which came under their power. Each of the planets had a characteristic nature and effect upon its subjects. Saturn, being cold and dry, encouraged melancholy; the hot dry planet Mars made choler predominate, and those born when the moon was in the ascendant would be phlegmatic in complexion. The planets were not, of course, all capable of influencing events at the same time. Even when it was above the horizon, a planet was not necessarily able to exert its power. Its position in the heavens, or the opposition of another planet, might neutralize its influence; and the prevailing sign of the zodiac might counteract the force of the planet. The task of calculating the final outcome of these different factors was part of the duty of the medieval physician, who could not treat his patient until he knew how the astrological influences were likely to affect the progress of the disease. A feverish patient would face a period of critical danger if Mars were in the ascendant, especially if he were a man of choleric complexion; and if Mars were about to enter a hot dry portion of the zodiac the patient's position would be desperate. Chaucer's Physician owes his remarkable eminence as a doctor to his skill in making such calculations. Whether in medicine or in surgery, Chaucer tells us, there 'was noon him lyk',

> For he was grounded in astronomye.[1]

It was not only the medical practitioner who needed such scientific knowledge. Throughout human affairs an ability to recognize the marks of planetary influence was vital to anyone whose profession demanded an expert judgement of other men, or of the likely course of future events.

We have seen that medieval astronomers recognized seven planets, circling the fixed body of the earth as satellites, and that the sun and the moon were counted as two of the seven. The others— Mercury, Venus, Mars, Jupiter and Saturn—were placed in this order, with Saturn furthest from the earth and the moon the nearest of the planets. The sun was given a position between Venus and Mars, as though attended by three planets on either side, 'in noble eminence enthroned and sphered'. Each of these celestial bodies had a distinctive character, and a power of influencing life on earth in a particular way; though this power might be qualified by the contrary effect of a neighbouring planet, or by its distance from the earth. Saturn, the most baleful and malefic of the seven, had least chance of bringing its destructive influence to bear because it was placed furthest off. Moreover, between Saturn and the earth stood Jupiter, a hot moist planet whose kindly aspect tempered the deadly force of his two neighbours, Mars and Saturn. The fiery, parched quality of Mars was in turn modified by the influence of the feminine planet Venus, whom a sixteenth-century writer was to describe as

a pacifier of Mars in his great fury and malice and fiery fervency, quieting him with friendly and amiable aspect in such wise as a beautiful and loving woman doth appease the rage of her husband.[2]

[1] The distinction between astronomy and astrology did not become effective until the seventeenth century.
[2] John Maplet, *The Dial of Destiny* (1581).

The second feminine planet was the moon, whose cold moist quality was transmitted to the earth as an influence which encouraged the growth of phlegmatic humours. This was counterbalanced by the influence of the sun, a planet whose heat was more temperate than the scorching fury of Mars, and whose distance from the earth softened the force which might otherwise injure living things. The physical arrangement of the planetary spheres bore witness to the wisdom of their creator, who had disposed them in such fashion that life on earth could not be overwhelmed by malefic influences, but was subjected in turn to a variety of forces—fortunate, hostile or indifferent.

We have seen that complexion or temperament was determined by a predominance of one of the four humours, and that this excess was the consequence of planetary influences affecting the constitution of the body. Mars dried up the moisture of the body and increased its heat, encouraging growth of choler. The parched, chilling effect of Saturn was to promote melancholy. The moon stimulated an increase of phlegm, and Venus—a warm moist planet—favoured the humour of blood and a sanguine complexion. These influences began to work upon the individual from the moment of his birth, sometimes combining to produce a character who displayed more than one of the planetary types. Where the influence was single and uncomplicated by other forces, it shaped a being whose whole nature—bodily, intellectual, temperamental and moral—bore the imprint of his natal planet. Those born under Venus, John Maplet explains,

are amiable and of a merry and smiling countenance, and their voice is very sweet or delectable. Their bodies are well set, and be of proper features; their faces and visages are round, their hair yellow, their eyes glittering and rolling. In conditions they be gentle, courteous, fair-spoken, mild and modest, meet for all companies.

We may recognize here some of the features of the lady Prioress, and realize that the inscription on her brooch has a particular aptness to the astrological type which Chaucer is slily revealing. The planetary influence which has determined the character of the Host, Harry

Bailly, is set down unmistakably in Chaucer's portrait. 'The sun', one of the great medieval authorities affirms, 'maketh a man corpulent, great of body, fair of face and well coloured, with great eyen.'[1] Chaucer refers to the Host's bodily size and prominent eyes in *The General Prologue*, and makes the Host himself allude to his corpulence when he calls Chaucer forward to tell a tale, commenting,

> He in the waast is shape as wel as I.

The masterful personality of the Host, which enables him to hold the pilgrims together 'in a flok' despite their individual diversity, might have been derived immediately from his planet. The same writer states his belief that the sun

> hath virtue of unity and accord, for he joineth, concileth and accordeth the planets in their own effects and doings. Also he accordeth together elements that be contrary.

The Host carries out the same function within the little world of the nine-and-twenty who admit his authority; and again like the sun, who rules 'with a good and favourable aspect', he gives encouragement and confidence to his subordinates, the pilgrims, making them 'to be of a courage indeed right manly, and very valiant' as they come forward with their tales. Another work on the planetary influences tells us that men born under the sun are often advanced to great honours and dignities. Chaucer's first comments on the Host pay respect to the qualities which fit him for high office. It may be worth recalling that the Harry Bailly of historical fact, whom Chaucer may have taken as the prototype of his Host, twice represented Southwark in Parliament, and also served as coroner, assessor, and controller of the subsidy for his borough.

The ugly, ferocious and dishonest Miller is evidently subject to Mars. He is identified first by his choleric temperament, seen in his bristly red hair and his violently aggressive behaviour, and then by the marks of coarse brutality and toughness stamped upon his appearance. Where those born under Venus are well-shaped and

---

[1] Bartholomaeus, *De proprietatibus rerum*, trans. Trevisa (1495).

attractive, like the Squire and the Prioress, the Miller is squat, massive and terrifying, with a gaping mouth and huge black nostrils. The sword and buckler which he carries reinforces the impression of a man dominated by Mars. The hot energy of this planet cannot combine with moisture to grow straight and graceful, but stunts and thickens the body, giving the Miller the unfeeling ferocity of a battering-ram. His personal tastes and his moral character are shaped by the same planetary influence. Those subject to Venus 'do greatly delight in music', as the Squire proves by singing and fluting all day long; but the Martialist enjoys coarser pleasures. His instrument is a squealing bagpipe, and his conversation is 'moost of sinne and harlotries'. The opinion of Bartholomaeus that Mars is 'red and untrue and guileful' is borne out in the Miller's cheating of his customers:

> Wel koude he stelen corn and tollen thries.

The qualities of wrath and boldness which he attributes to the Martialist are illustrated by the Miller's behaviour as soon as the pilgrimage gets under way. Contemptuous of social precedence, he rudely thrusts himself upon the company at the end of *The Knight's Tale*, and then quarrels with the Reeve over the choice of a story, designed to ridicule another carpenter. John Maplet completes the identification of the Miller as a Martialist by commenting on the angry impetuousness of this planetary type, describing such men as 'wild and savage rather than properly puissant; and more venturous-rash and bold than considerate and politic'. The Reeve appears at first to be another choleric character, with the spare, gaunt body of a man whose flesh has been parched and consumed by inward heat. In other respects, however, the Reeve exhibits the cold dry quality which characterizes melancholy and the planetary influence of Saturn. This ambiguousness of complexion is explained by the fact that the Reeve is an old man. 'Ik am oold', he admits in the prologue to his Tale,

> This white top writeth mine olde yeris;
> Myn herte is also mowled as mine heris.[1]

[1] 'My vital spirit has become as worn-out as my hair.'

In the period of old age the blood flowed sluggishly through the veins, the moisture of the organs and tissues dried up, and the vital heat of the body abated. Accordingly the heat of choler grew cold though remaining dry, and the choleric complexion shifted to melancholic. Thus a man not born under Saturn came under the influence of this planet as his body acquired the same cold dry quality, and eventually died because it could no longer supply the warmth and moisture needed to nourish his vital spirits. Where the choleric man would be recognized by his raging fury, the Reeve's behaviour reveals the hard dry malice of a person who shares the hostility of Saturn towards every form of life. 'They were adrad of him as of the deeth', Chaucer tells us of the Reeve's subordinates; and whether he is referring to the terrible plague of 1348 or to death itself, the comment associates the Reeve firmly with the planet whose influence is 'dry, malicious and hurtful'. His lonely dwelling-place on the heath, and his habit of separating himself from the other pilgrims by riding last in the cavalcade, help to confirm the Reeve's affinity with Saturn. 'Solitariness is a great part of their desire', John Maplet remarks of Saturnists; and he refers to the example of Timon of Athens, who 'through a waywardness and crookedness of nature, abhorred and shunned all men's companies'. Unlike the Mercurial man, the Saturnist has no intellectual quickness and finds learning difficult, but what he manages to master is permanently lodged in his mind. This characteristic seems to be reflected in the Reeve's expert knowledge of all the affairs of the estate, and his meticulous management of accounts. Although not an educated man, he has learned all that appertains to his duties, and keeps all this stored-up information and experience at the front of his narrowly suspicious mind, overlooking nothing. His position at the tail of the pilgrimage, bearing the 'rusty blade' which symbolizes both his age and his malice, corresponds to the position of the planet which rules him.

The Wife of Bath is an example of the blended character produced by the influence of two planets. She herself recognizes and frankly admits this double affinity:

For certes, I am al Venerien
In feelinge, and myn herte is Marcien.
Venus me yaf my lust, my likerousnesse,[1]
And Mars yaf me my sturdy hardinesse.

It is Venus who has led her into five marriages and the youthful indiscretions which Chaucer tactfully leaves undisclosed, and who inspires the Wife's shameless defence of sexual pleasure in the prologue to her Tale. A lover of company, fine clothes, gossip and merriment, she is easily identified as a woman bearing the imprint of 'seinte Venus seel'; but comparison with the demure Prioress shows that the Wife's noisily flamboyant and overbearing manner must have some other planetary source. What the Wife calls hardiness—her bold audacity, evident in her scarlet stockings as in her startling freedom of speech—comes from the influence of Mars. Some of the features of her portrait, such as her sharp spurs and the hat which suggests 'a bokeler or a targe', isolate the Martialist element in her double personality; but for the most part the two influences combine with grotesquely comic effect. The characteristic influence of Venus is still discernible, but distorted and vulgarized by the masculine qualities which the Wife derives from her second planet. The fondness for elegant dress which Venus gives to her subjects becomes exaggerated into a taste for loud and ostentatious display lacking all feminine reserve: scarlet gytes or gowns, coverchiefs weighing ten pounds, and enormous hats. The temperamental aptness for love which Chaucer sees so delicately implicit in the Prioress's soft red mouth is similarly overstated in the Wife through the headstrong energy of Mars. After exhausting five husbands she is still sexually insatiable, and looking for a sixth partner on whom to bestow 'the beste quoniam mighte be'. Her account of her marital adventures is as brazenly direct as her style of dress. She exposes the most intimately feminine of experiences to a fascinated audience without any sense of modesty or restraint, denying herself the mysteriousness of a woman and insisting that the greatest desire

---

[1] 'licentiousness'.

of her sex is to dominate the male. Her passionate determination to wrest the mastery or 'soveraynetee' from her husband is the conclusive mark of her Martialist character. Against the pleasure-loving gaiety and promiscuousness that the Wife derives from Venus, her loud voice, widely spaced teeth and broad-hipped solidity all speak of the influence of Mars. Her second planet has implanted in her a love of conquest more powerful than the deep-seated sexual appetite which rules her body.

But the planetary influences do not completely account for the Wife of Bath's character and temperament. When she tells her audience,

> Myn ascendent was Taur, and Mars therinne,

she refers to one of the associated influences which affected the force of the natal planet, and so of the disposition which it helped to form. The setting of the heavens, against which the planets moved, was not a blank but a region coloured by influences as potent as those of the planets themselves. The great celestial sphere which was the apparent orbit of the sun formed the centre of a band within which the movements of the planets took place. We know now that this band, some eighteen degrees wide, represents an observer's view of the solar system from the earth as it makes its yearly revolution about the sun. This circular movement brings different portions of the heavens into view throughout the year, so that the observer on earth sees different constellations of stars moving successively across the sky within the band of the ecliptic. By dividing this band into twelve sections, and assigning one particular constellation to each in order of their annual sequence, the ancient astronomers produced the zodiac. The sections were known as signs, and the beginning of each originally coincided with the appearance of the constellation above the horizon. Chaucer's *Treatise on the Astrolabe* shows that in his lifetime this occurred about the twelfth or thirteenth day of the month. The appearance of Aries or the Ram in March was taken as the beginning of the year. The Canterbury pilgrims set out soon afterwards, when

> the yonge sonne
> Hath in the Ram his halve cours yronne;

that is, at a date somewhere between 27 March and 12 April, when the sun entered the sign of Taurus, the Bull.

Then followed in order the signs of Gemini, Cancer, Leo, Virgo, Libra, Scorpio, Sagittarius, Capricornus, Aquarius and Pisces.[1] Their names gave each of the signs a distinctive character, and suggested the prevailing temper of the period during which they were above the horizon. The elemental qualities of fiery, earthy, airy and watery were ascribed to the signs in regular succession, so that the quality of every fifth sign was alike. Thus the fiery sign Aries was followed four months later by the fiery sign Leo, and after another four months by the third fiery sign, Sagittarius. Taurus, an earthy sign, was followed after the same interval by Virgo and then by Capricornus, which both shared its earthy quality; and the airy signs, Gemini, Libra and Aquarius, recurred in the same way.

Because they heralded a change of season, Aries, Cancer, Libra and Capricornus were known as cardinal or moveable signs, and an appropriate complexion was ascribed to each. Aries introduced spring, and was considered a warm moist sign. Cancer, which appeared at the onset of summer, was hot and dry; Libra brought in autumn with cold and dry, and Capricornus winter with its cold moist sign. Under these four cardinal signs the complexions of all living things were strengthened and renewed. In each of the zodiacal months following—that is to say, under the signs of Taurus, Leo, Scorpio and Aquarius—the complexions remained constant. For this reason they were named the fixed signs, and the remaining four— Gemini, Virgo, Sagittarius and Pisces—were described as common signs, under whose influence the complexions declined in strength. Thus, during every period of four months each of the elemental qualities enjoyed its time of predominance in the zodiac; and during the three months of every season the four complexions varied in strength as the signs changed, beginning strongly under the cardinal

[1] The Twins, the Crab, the Lion, the Virgin, the Balance, the Scorpion, the Archer, the Goat, the Water-carrier, the Fishes.

sign, moderating as the fixed sign rose, and becoming weak under the common sign during the third part of the season.

As each of the signs occupied one-twelfth part of the heavens, or thirty degrees, six of them were passing across the sky at any given time; three rising towards the zenith, and three declining towards the western horizon. A sign exerted its greatest influence when it was in the ascendant; that is, just rising above the eastern horizon. Consequently, as Chaucer observes in his treatise, the ascendant, 'as wel in all nativites as in questions and eleccions of times, is a thing which that these astrologiens gretly observen'. This portion of the ecliptic, with the sign and the planet passing through it at the moment of a person's birth, was the crucial influence upon his individual temperament and the course of his personal fortunes. For purposes of astrological calculation it was necessary to know the year as well as the day and month of birth, for while the signs returned annually at the same time of year, the individual planets took varying lengths of time to complete their orbits. Mars, for instance, made one revolution every two years; so that if he were in Pisces at one given time, a year later he would be found in opposition to this sign, in Virgo. Jupiter required twelve years for his revolution, and so moved from one sign to the next during the course of the year. What influence a particular planet could exert depended upon the sign in which it appeared. Mercury, Venus, Mars, Jupiter and Saturn had each two houses in which the planet was judged at home, and able to influence events. The sun and the moon had a single house each, Leo and Cancer respectively. The houses of Mercury were Gemini and Virgo, those of Venus were Libra and Taurus, and Aries and Scorpio were assigned to Mars. In addition each planet was associated with a third sign, called its exaltation, by which its influence was magnified. The exaltation of Mars was Capricornus, Jupiter had its exaltation in Cancer, and the sun—as the Squire reminds his audience—acquired special force through his exaltation in Aries:

> Phebus the sonne ful joly was and cleer;
> For he was neigh his exaltacioun

In Martes face, and in his mansioun
In Aries, the colerik hoote signe.[1]

The Squire's reminder that Aries is 'the colerik hoote signe' explains why this house encourages the sun to exert her greatest influence. The planet and the sign share the same hot dry quality, and so its environment intensifies the force of the planet. Conversely, when the sun is in Libra its planetary influence is checked by the opposite qualities of the sign. Such a house, where the influence of a planet was at its weakest, was called its depression. Venus had her exaltation in Pisces and her depression in Virgo, an earthy sign which counteracted her own hot moist influence.

These facts help to account for the curious temperament implanted in the Wife of Bath. She was born, she tells the pilgrims, when Taurus had just appeared above the horizon, with Mars in the house of the ascendant. Taurus being one of the houses of Venus, the influence of the sign was responsible for her gaiety and wantonness. Had Venus herself been in the ascendant instead of Mars, the Wife would have received the beauty and gracefulness proper to a woman. Unluckily, the influence which Venus would have exerted through her sign was intercepted by the malignant planet Mars, and although his evil aspect was subdued by Venus while he remained in her house,[2] the Wife's immodesty, her self-assertiveness and her sturdy figure all bear witness to the diverting of Venus's influence by Mars. Her gap-toothed mouth and bold red face suggest physical affinities with the terrifying god of war which her enthusiasm for life and adventure cannot conceal.

To calculate a horoscope exactly it was necessary to know the time as well as the date of birth, for the planetary influences changed

[1] Each sign was divided into three parts, extending over ten degrees and called faces. Beside being the exaltation of the sun, Aries—as mentioned above—was one of the houses of Mars. For this reason the first ten degrees of Aries were known as the face of Mars; in the Squire's phrase, 'Martes face'. When the Canterbury pilgrims set out the sun had run 'his halve cours' in Aries, and was situated in the second face of the sign, the face of the sun.

[2] See *Troilus and Criseyde*, III, 22, where the poet extols this power in Venus: 'Ye fierse Mars apaisen [mitigate] his ire'.

from hour to hour. For astrological purposes the period between sunrise and sunset, and the subsequent period of darkness, were both divided into twelve 'hours inequal'; so called because except at the equinoxes a diurnal and a nocturnal hour were not of the same length. Each of these hours was governed by one of the planets; the first by the planet whose day it was, and the others following in order descending through the spheres. Thus on Friday the first hour after sunrise belonged to Venus, the second to Mercury, the third to the moon, the fourth to Saturn, and so on. By this reckoning the twenty-fourth hour belonged to the moon, and the inequal hours of Saturday began after sunrise with an hour appropriately governed by Saturn. By the end of Saturday the sequence of planets had brought round Mars, and Sunday began as it should with a first hour dominated by its own planet, the sun.[1] The eighth, fifteenth and twenty-second hours of every day came under the influence of its planet as well as the first hour. These four periods, two during the day and two after sunset, were the times most favourable for transacting any business in which the influence of the planet would be helpful. For this reason the three suppliants in *The Knight's Tale* make their prayers for success at different hours before and after sunrise on Monday. By astrological reckoning it is still Sunday when Palamon goes to the temple of Venus 'in hir houre' before sunrise, when 'it nere nat day by houres two'. The twenty-second hour of Sunday belonged to the planet of the day, and the next was therefore dominated by Venus. This is the moment, two inequal hours before sunrise, when Palamon's prayers are most likely to prosper. At the beginning of the 'thridde houre inequal' after this,

Up roos the sonne, and up roos Emelie

to make her appeal to the goddess of chastity in the temple of Diana. The planet of this goddess is the moon, and as Monday has now

[1] Why the twenty-fifth hour should bring round the appropriate planet may not be immediately obvious. But if the days of the week are set out in the order of their planetary affinity—Saturday, Thursday, Tuesday, Sunday, Friday, Wednesday, Monday—a forward count of twenty-four places from any particular day always ends on the day falling next in the normal weekly sequence.

173

begun the first hour of the day comes under her domination. Emily's petition is unsuccessful because, as the goddess explains, the gods have decreed that she must marry one of her two suitors, and the planet cannot override this decision; but Emily has chosen the hour of her appeal correctly. Arcite's prayer to the god of arms and battle follows at

The nexte houre of Mars folwinge this.

Chaucer does not tell us at what time this occurs; but as the first hour belongs to the moon, Mars would have his first period of influence after the hours of Saturn and Jupiter; that is, during the fourth hour after sunrise. His prayer is successful, and when the combat takes place on Tuesday—Mars's own day—Arcite is victorious. However, the cause of Venus and Palamon has been taken under the protection of Saturn; and as Arcite gallops through the lists as victor, a 'furie infernal' breaks out of the ground in front of his horse. This apparition, sent by Pluto 'at requeste of Saturne', causes the horse to throw Arcite, who is fatally injured. Saturn has chosen his time well: immediately after sunset on Tuesday, and so the thirteenth inequal hour of a day whose planetary sequence began with Mars and has now brought round Saturn. His nature, as he has explained to Venus earlier in the tale, gives him a particular affinity with fatal accidents and violent death:

Myn is the drenching[1] in the see so wan;
Myn is the prison in the derke cote;[2]
Myn is the strangling and hanging by the throte.

The hour which strengthens Saturn's influence also increases the likelihood of injury and death through accidents such as the god deliberately contrives.

The astrological hours had an obvious importance in the practice of medicine. The skilled physician administered treatment during the hour whose planet could be expected to assist the action of the drug or to strengthen the affected part of the body. This explains Chaucer's remark about his Physician, who 'kepte his pacient a ful

---

[1] 'drowning'. [2] 'dungeon'.

greet deel in houres'; carefully watching for the most auspicious moment to apply his remedies. His treatment would take into account the varying strength of the individual humours of the body during the natural day. During the six hours following midnight the humour of blood had dominion. For the next six hours the dominant humour was choler. Melancholy had its period of greatest strength from midday until six o'clock, and during the remaining period up to midnight phlegm was abundant. Each portion of the day constituted a potential danger-period for the patient whose illness was caused by, or associated with, an excess of the humour which predominated during those six hours; for during that period the over-abundant humour would be still further enlarged. On the other hand, during the remaining period of six hours which made up the half-day the contrary humour was predominant; the six sanguine hours being followed by the period of melancholic abundance, and the choleric hours of the afternoon having as medical counterpoise the phlegmatic period of evening and early night. Thus the dangerous hours were offset by a period whose predominant humour helped the physician in his attempts to restore the healthy balance of bodily fluids. If a planetary hour within that period offered to strengthen this neutralizing effect—as when the inequal hour of Mars fell within the choleric afternoon period, strengthening the opposition to a phlegmatic disease—the moment to begin medical treatment was more precisely defined.

Other planetary factors did not fall so readily within the medieval physician's area of control. The onset of a disease followed a conjunction of influences harmful to the patient, by studying which—and especially the position and state of the moon—the physician was able to diagnose the cause of the sickness. As the planetary dispositions changed, their malefic influence might gradually diminish and allow the body to regain its healthy balance; but the physician had rather to expect a worsening of the illness as the baleful conjunction strengthened its position in the ascendant. The aspect of an auspicious planet such as Jupiter or Venus could reduce the danger:

if not, as the malefic planet rose it might move into a sign which increased its power to the point where medical remedies became useless. If, for instance, during the course of a disease induced by the phlegmatic influence of the moon, the planet moved from Gemini to Cancer, the illness would take a firmer hold on the patient; for in the watery sign of Cancer the moon is in her own house, and has her greatest power of producing cold moist humours. The patient could be helped by the contrary aspect of a hot dry planet in opposition—that is, 180 degrees distant; but this would be in Capricornus, a cold moist sign whose effect would qualify the helpful influence of the planet. Although the physician could discover through calculation the approach of critical hours, and the most favourable times for applying remedies, he could not hope to neutralize the planetary forces which brought the disease about, and which would probably determine its eventual outcome.[1]

In the view of medieval medicine, death supervened when the bodily spirits became unable to stimulate the vital functions, either through their own weakness or by reason of some fatal obstruction of one of the bodily powers. Sir Thomas Elyot follows established tradition in describing spirit as 'an ayry substance subtyll' which stirs the powers of the body to perform their functions;[2] and a writer later in the same century gives a more graphic account of its activity. 'This spirit', he affirms,

is the chief instrument and immediate whereby the soul bestoweth the exercises of her faculty in her body, that passeth to and fro in a moment, nothing in swiftness and nimbleness being comparable thereunto.[3]

In this way medieval science accounted for activities and sensations which are now attributed to the central nervous system, with its headquarters in the brain. Medieval authorities distinguished three

---

[1] For a detailed account of the play of planetary influences upon the progress of a particular illness, see Curry, *Chaucer and the Medieval Sciences* (revised ed. 1960), pp. 14–19.

[2] *The Castle of Health* (1541).

[3] Timothy Bright, *A Treatise of Melancholy* (1586). The passage is reproduced in *The Frame of Order*, edited by the present writer (1957), p. 57.

kinds of spirit, each with a different location in one of the organs of the body. The purest and most volatile was animal spirit, so called on account of its affinity with the *anima* or soul of man. This had its seat in the brain, and was distributed about the body by the sinews, giving power of movement and sensation. Next in importance came vital spirit, which from its seat in the heart was conveyed through the arteries to enliven all the members of the body. The last was natural spirit, whose seat was in the liver, the source of physical nourishment and growth; and this was dispersed through the veins along with the nutriment which the liver had converted into blood. The circulation of the blood was to remain unknown until the discovery made by William Harvey, and published in his *De circulatione sanguinis* in 1628. The medieval physiologists followed Galen in believing there to be two kinds of blood, natural and vital, each flowing in its own closed system of arteries or of veins. 'The veins beareth the nourishing blood', writes Richard Copland, 'and the arteries the spiritual blood. For the veins breed of the liver, and the arteries of the heart.'[1] Before Harvey's discovery, the heart was considered not as a pump sending the blood round the body but, in Copland's phrase, as 'a very hot burning oven', from which heat and vital spirits spread outwards along the arteries, to warm and vivify all the members.

Each of the three spirits was assigned a distinct function. The first provided animal power. This was seen in such intellectual activities as discerning, judging and invention, in voluntary movement, and in the faculty of sensation exercised through the five wits. According to Elyot, that part of animal power responsible for determining individual actions induced three mental faculties: imagination in the forehead, reason in the brain, and remembrance in the noddle, or back of the head. Here as elsewhere Elyot is following established opinion as declared by medieval doctors from the eleventh century onwards. A modern writer summarizes this agreement about the functions of the three parts of the brain:

The Questionary of Surgeons (1542).

The first is fantastic, from which the senses are controlled, where the sensations are registered, and where the process of imagination goes on. The middle cell is logical or rational, and there the forms received from the senses and imagination are examined and judged. The third cell retains such forms as pass this examination and so is the seat of memory.[1]

The function of vital power was to promote the action of the heart, lungs and other essential organs, while natural power carried out the processes of nutrition and assimilation. Stimulated by the spirits, these various powers kept body and mind alert and in a vigorous state of health, which began to fail when injury to the body, or their own weakness, prevented them from carrying out their duties. When the Player-King in *Hamlet* warns his Queen,

My operant powers their functions leave to do;

he is making a quite specific reference to his physiological condition, in terms which Chaucer's audience would have understood in the same sense. With increasing age the spirits became enfeebled, and unable to stimulate the activity of the bodily organs upon which life depended.

Among its particular duties, natural spirit impelled four bodily functions of special concern to the medieval physician: appetite, retention, digestion and expulsion. Like the humours, they were associated with pairs of qualities, so that digestion required heat and moisture, and retention cold and dryness. As with the humours, it was necessary to maintain a balance between the four activities; not allowing the body to become exhausted by inordinate losses, nor choked with unexpelled matter. The obvious importance of these functions was strengthened by the belief that, since the spirits took their origin from the digestive process, any organic failure here would have serious consequences throughout the body. Natural spirit was extracted from food during digestion, 'being made of the purest aliment in the liver'; and from this substance the more volatile vital spirit was derived. This in turn, after a further stage of

[1] L. Thorndike, *History of Magic and Experimental Science* (1923), I, 660.

refining and purifying, was transformed into animal spirit. For this reason, as a Dutch writer of the sixteenth century argued,

it standeth us upon to use the most exquisite diet that may be, to the end that the meats and nourishments, being laboured into good and whole-some juice, may make the spirits pure, sincere and perfect.[1]

This assured that only agreeable vapours would be sent up into the brain, where they would 'marvellously comfort and clarify the instruments of the senses'. The greater the clarity and subtlety of the animal spirit, the more readily did it lend itself to intellectual activity; but when the digestive process was disturbed, or bad food was taken into the stomach, only coarse spirits could reach the brain. In such cases, Lemnius explains, the crude humours contained in the food

be not sufficiently and enough concocted and attentuate, and unpure spirits proceed out of them, enforcing a manifest alteration of the state as well of the body as of the mind.

Thus the consequences of a poor digestion were seen in mental dull-ness as well as in the blotches and skin-eruptions caused by impure spirits within the body. Good health required the power of ridding the body of such corrupting influences, whether spirits or material substances. This was the function of the virtue expulsive, as one medieval writer describes this faculty; 'which expelleth and putteth away that that is unconvenient and hurtful to kind', meaning to human nature. A person who had lost this virtue or power would be unable to clear his lungs of matter accumulating from a disease, or from an injury which caused the blood to rot in his veins. Arcite dies from this cause. As Chaucer explains,

> The vertu expulsif, or animal,
> Fro thilke vertu cleped natural
> Ne may the venym voyden ne expelle.

The passage shows that although the faculty of expulsion should be exercised by the natural power, where there was some physical

[1] Lemnius, *Touchstone of Complexions*, trans. Newton (1565).

disability this faculty would be taken over by the superior force of animal virtue, located in the brain. In Arcite's case the animal power is as helpless as the natural, for 'every lacerte [muscle] in his brest adoun' is poisoned by corrupted blood, and unable to respond to any stimulus. Prevented from coughing, he cannot expel the clotted blood from his lungs, which oppresses the heart and eventually extinguishes the vital spirits. The onset of death in Arcite, as in Falstaff, is shown by the withdrawing of vital heat from the extremities as the spirits rally to the support of the heart:

> For from his feet up to his brest was come
> The coold of deeth, that hadde him overcome,
> And yet mooreover,[1] for in his armes two
> The vital strengthe is lost and all ago.

The physician recognizes the hopelessness of the case, and gives up the struggle to maintain his patient's life.

In such a desperate situation a medieval physician might have wished for the fabulous elixir which was to cure all diseases and prolong natural life. This was one of three substances, usually called stones and endowed with magical properties, whose manufacture remained a scientific dream over several centuries. The first was to be a universal remedy and preservative which, providing he avoided accidents, would confer immortality upon its possessor. This was known as *lapis vegetabilis*, or the vegetable stone. The second, *lapis animalis*, was to have the effect of making all the senses keenly perceptive. The third, the mineral stone, would have the power of purifying and transmuting base metals into silver and gold. As we might expect, this last prospect proved far more attractive than the other two, and the term 'the philosophers' stone', although applicable to all three, came to be used only of the great elixir which was to transmute lead into silver, and copper into gold.

The Canon's Yeoman's Tale, like Ben Jonson's play *The Alchemist* two centuries later, shows how the hope of transmuting base metals was made a bait for the greedy and credulous, who were persuaded

---

[1] 'still further'.

to finance the expensive process that was to make them millionaires. Despite this abuse, alchemy began as a scientific study, based on assumptions about the nature and composition of substances that were as serious as the molecular theory of our own times. Gold was regarded not merely as the heaviest and most precious of metals, but as the noblest of substances; enjoying a place in the created hierarchy corresponding to that of the sun among the planets, or of the king among his subjects and lords. This encouraged a belief that the other metals differed from one another in terms of absolute worth—silver being of greater dignity than copper, and tin being above lead in the scale of created values. Thus it could be assumed that the metals beneath gold in the hierarchy represented intermediate stages in the production of this most exalted substance. They had failed to reach the state of gold because their constituent elements had not been sufficiently refined and concentrated to attain this culminating degree of noble purity. 'Lead and other metals', the alchemist argues in Jonson's play, 'would be gold if they had time'; and he declares it absurd

> To think that nature in the earth bred gold
> Perfect in the instant: something went before.

This something was a baser metal which the warmth of the earth would, in time, bring to perfection. The alchemist's task was to accelerate this tedious process of development by heat and distillation, treating a curious mixture of ingredients—designed to include every form of natural substance—until they yielded the essential matter of gold.

The alchemists recognized seven metals, corresponding with the seven planets. The Canon's Yeoman sets out the correspondences, as well as reciting a long list of alchemical ingredients:

> Sol gold is, and Luna silver we threpe,[1]
> Mars iren, Mercurie quiksilver we clepe,
> Saturnus leed, and Juppiter is tin,
> And Venus coper, by my fader kin!

[1] 'affirm'.

With the help of the so-called spirits listed by this pilgrim—
'arsenik, sal armoniak, and brimstoon'—and the heat of a charcoal
fire, the alchemist submitted his ingredients to seven stages of treatment: distillation, congellation, solution, descension, sublimation,
calcination and fixation. The resulting elixir, he hoped, would be the
philosophers' stone: itself the highest exaltation of material substance, and capable of transmuting base metal into gold merely by
touch. Repeated disappointment and failure could not shake
medieval faith in the practical possibility of manufacturing this
entirely mythical substance. Greed had something to do with the
persistence of the alchemists' dream, but their belief was supported
by scientific principles which could not be discredited by experimental proof. Failure was ascribed to technical difficulties or errors
of calculation; and where the metals had affinities with the seven
planets, there was a constant problem of securing the most favourable influences to assist projection. These complications, together
with the involved task of blending ingredients in the correct
proportions—

> Sal tartre, alkaly, and sal preparat,
> And combust materes and coagulat;
> Cley maad with hors or mannes heer, and oille
> Of tartre, alum glas, berme, wort, and argoille[1]

—exposed the alchemist to the possibility of failure at every stage of
the process. Repeated disappointment did not force him to realize
that the philosophers' stone was a myth, but indicated that his
calculations had gone astray.

It is easy to assume a condescending attitude towards medieval
science and those who practised it, and to ridicule the credulity
which allowed otherwise intelligent men to accept such unlikely
explanations of the phenomena about them. Skeat, one of the best-
informed of Chaucer's editors, himself scoffs at many of the scientific
ideas which he interprets for modern readers, objecting that the

[1] For an explanatory comment see the note on lines 810–13 of *The Canon's
Yeoman's Tale* in Maurice Hussey's edition (Cambridge, 1965).

medieval mind attributes qualities to natural forces and concepts in a completely arbitrary way. The charge is undeserved. Granted its initial premises—of four elements and humours, sharing the qualities of hot and cold, dry and moist, of seven planets and twelve signs—medieval science builds up its detailed structure of relationships with consistent logic. It may seem difficult to understand how a purely fabulous substance such as choler could have been accepted as the basis of medical diagnosis, or accredited with qualities which gave it close affinity with the equally fanciful sign of Cancer and the essential element of fire. To a modern mind, none of these ideas has any correspondence with fact. But a medieval scientist could not reject the concept of four elements without calling into question the whole fabric of contemporary belief. If there were not four elements, the four humours derived from them must also be non-existent, and the whole study of physiology and medicine would be undermined. Further, since there would be no means of accounting for the planetary influences—themselves sharing the elemental attributes of hot and dry, and their opposites—astronomy too would be discredited. The interlocking system of ideas was too close and interdependent for any single part to be withdrawn. The old philosophy could only be discarded when scientific inquiry had grown bold enough to question the central authority of Aristotle, Ptolemy, Galen and others, whose opinions dominated scientific thought for nearly two thousand years, and inventive enough to propose an entirely new method of explaining the nature of things.

During Chaucer's lifetime this point lay still too far ahead to be foreseen. His mind explores the curious world of medieval scientific belief with lively interest and credulity. His attitude is not difficult to understand. However naïve and absurd the assumptions of medieval science, its conception of universal order was never impersonal or abstruse. The principles of natural life could be expressed in plain terms of human experience, of heat and moisture, growth and decay, likeness and antipathy, and of genial and malefic influences. The working of this great natural system could be

understood without recourse to the involved mathematical calculations upon which modern scientific knowledge depends. A medieval
scientist would have had no means of applying them to a world
which he was not concerned to weigh or to measure. He saw natural
objects obeying impulses as simple and direct as the likes and dislikes
of human beings, and reaching conclusions through a contest of
forces no more complicated than these elementary feelings. Man
could feel himself surrounded and acted upon by powers which
shared his own nature, to the extent of moving under the same kind
of prompting, and answering the same stimulus of sympathy or
revulsion. He was not abandoned in the numbing vacancy of a
universe unable to acknowledge his existence, such as modern science
depicts, but stood at the centre of things, the focus of all created life.
Everything was accounted for. Much in medieval life must have
been grim and uncomfortable; but against this the scientific beliefs
of the age offered a sense of intimate involvement in a universal
design which gave shape and purpose to man's experience. We may
feel ourselves participating in this intellectual assurance when we
read Chaucer's poetry.

APPENDIX:
SOME DIFFICULT WORDS

A number of words which occur frequently in Chaucer's writings are difficult not simply because we now use different words for the same things but because they have no exact modern equivalents at all. In some cases this is so because the words are the names of things which are no longer part of our lives, such as parts of medieval costume—*habergeoun* or *coverchief*—or items of medieval food and drink—*mortreux* or *claree*. Here the only difficulty is to identify and imagine the thing referred to. In other cases a word is difficult because it is the name not of a thing but of a concept belonging to some system of ideas no longer current; and here the problem is likely to be greater. Sometimes, in order to understand such a word, we shall have to learn something of a particular medieval science. Thus, in order to understand what Chaucer means by *complexioun*, we shall have to find out that, according to the physiology of his day, the human system was governed by four *humours*, and that the proportion of these in a particular individual made up his *complexioun*—'disposition' is the nearest modern equivalent, but it does not imply, as *complexioun* does, the direct dependence of psychology on physiology. But even here, the difficulty can be overcome with relative ease, for medieval physiology is a fairly exact science, and so *complexioun* has a definite and tangible meaning. The same is true of even more abstruse sciences whose terminology Chaucer frequently uses, such as astrology and alchemy. The greatest difficulty comes with the names of concepts connected with larger and less definable medieval systems of ideas—ideas of the nature of man and his position in the universe. In such cases, we still use the words (as indeed we do in the case of *complexioun*), but as conceptions of man and the world have changed, the words have gradually shifted in meaning, until, in their modern form, they may be a positive barrier to our understanding. Here one may mention *nature*, *vertu*, *wit* and *corage*: all are extant in modern English, but for an understanding of how they are used by Chaucer, some knowledge of the medieval 'world-picture' is necessary. There are again—and these are perhaps trickiest of all—ethical terms, words used in the judgement of human conduct. Here there may be less chance of our misunderstanding inadvertently, for some of these terms are the subject of explicit discussion in Chaucer's works: *The Wife of Bath's Tale*, for example, includes a long speech on the true meaning of *gentillesse* (roughly, 'nobility'), while *The Franklin's Tale* invites us to consider true and false estimates of the same quality, and also of a closely related quality, *franchise*. But for their meaning such words depend not on definite intellectual systems, but on vaguer assumptions about human life and conduct, assumptions which are sometimes indeed unformulated. Thus a little more needs to be said here about the social background to medieval ethical terms, since it is from this background that the words draw their strength.

Democratic ideals played little part in medieval thought about society. Society was divided into distinct classes or estates, and these were organized hierarchically, though according to more than one hierarchy. Thus the hierarchy of family produces a distinction between *gentil* and *vileyn*, while the hierarchy of learning produces one between *clerk* (or *lered*) and *lewed*, and these two hierarchies do not necessarily correspond—there were men of high birth who could not read, and learned men who behaved like *vileyns*. Chaucer's terms for human conduct are derived from these hierarchies, but this is not to say that he supposed that 'noblemen' always behaved 'nobly'. Indeed the burden of the discussion of *gentillesse* in *The Wife of Bath's Tale* is that true *gentillesse* is shown not in a man's birth but in his actual behaviour: it is derived not from one's ancestors but from God. This thought was a medieval commonplace. The correspondence between class and conduct was an ideal, not necessarily a reality, and this makes Chaucer's language of moral judgement flexible and subtle. Our best guide to this language, and to the other difficult words in Chaucer, is simply a repeated and pondered reading of his works. As a modern critic has written:

It is only by coming across particular words...again and again in the various living and changing contexts of Chaucer's poetry that the reader begins to acquire a feeling for their specifically Chaucerian shades of meaning and implications, a feeling more delicate and exact than he would get by providing himself with modern equivalents from a glossary or notes.[1]

But a modern reader may get a helpful start in this reading from some preliminary explanation, so long as he realizes that this explanation cannot hope to provide an exact 'translation' of Chaucer's terminology.

Cherl See *Vileyn*.

Clerk The wide prevalence of illiteracy in medieval society meant that to be able to read was then a far greater distinction than it is now. The word *clerk* is used by Chaucer in its lowest sense to mean simply someone who can read, but it may also imply greater learning. It may be applied to a student, or to a learned man—we still use 'scholar' to refer both to someone who is still learning and to someone who is already learned. In these senses the opposite of *clerk* was *lewed*: illiterate, unlearned, ignorant (*not* the modern 'lewd'). *Lered* (learned) is also used as a conveniently alliterating antonym of *lewed*. But since literacy and the learning it made possible had in the earlier Middle Ages been confined almost entirely to persons in clerical orders, the word *clerk* was also used to denote such a person (that is to say, a priest or a member of minor orders). This was the word's original sense in Latin and French, from which the other senses mentioned above gradually developed.

Corage The modern meaning of courage—valour, bravery—is found as a meaning of *corage* in the Middle Ages, but it also possessed other meanings that have now been lost. In *The Merchant's Tale* we read that Januarie had 'a greet corage to been a wedded man', and here the primary meaning is a general inclination of mind. Since the heart (Latin *cor*, French *cœur*) was considered to be the seat of the feelings in general, the word in English also assumed a wider range of emotions than it can now cover. *Corage* could mean love, for instance, or lust,

[1] John Speirs, in *The Age of Chaucer*, ed. Boris Ford (Penguin Books, 1954), p. 24.

and by a further extension in meaning it could come to mean a man's sexual powers or sexual prowess. In another direction it was extended to stand for the violent passion of anger.

Curteys This is similar in meaning to *Gentil* (see below), but more specialized, since it implies not simply high birth but familiarity with the elegant behaviour current in the courts of rulers. Thus it lays more stress on the externals of behaviour—deference to others particularly— but also on devotion to women. A major leisure activity of medieval courtly society was *fine amour* or *amour courtois*, a 'game of love' according to which a man would devote himself to a woman, for whom his real feelings might be more or less serious, and take her as his 'lady', in a relationship which reversed the normal medieval dominance of the male (in marriage, for example). *Curteysye* might also be conceived of in heavenly terms, with the Blessed Virgin as the object of devotion, but this is less common in Chaucer. Thus *curteysye* possessed a wide spectrum of meanings, ranging from good manners or politeness (the modern 'courtesy') to accomplished devotion to the love of women, or a woman.

Daunger See *Pitee*.

Franchise (adj. *Free*) Like *curteysye*, *franchise* is a word linked with *gentillesse*, but it is specialized in a different direction, that of generosity or self-disregard. Like *curteysye*, it may be applied in a whole range of senses, from the generous mediation of the Blessed Virgin to mere open-handedness with money. *The Franklin's Tale* takes the form of a competition in *franchise* between a knight, a squire and a scholar. Thus a term which originally had a social meaning (for *free* originally referred to the status of freedom as opposed to servility) can be detached from its social context and used in an almost purely ethical sense; though perhaps it is worth noting that knights, squires, and scholars would all be *free* in both senses.

Gentillesse This is a very general term, used most frequently to refer to the kind of behaviour that one would expect of a person of high birth and breeding: noble, gracious, courteous, generous. But it may also be used in an exclusively social sense: the *gentils* among the Canterbury pilgrims who approve of *The Knight's Tale* are those of higher social rank, not necessarily those who themselves behave in the appropriate way. The discussion of *gentillesse*, also called *gentrye*, in *The Wife of Bath's Tale* (1109–76) will be found helpful, as will Chaucer's *balade* on the subject.

Honest This word has changed in meaning by becoming more specialized since Chaucer's day. Chaucer uses it to mean 'decent' or reliable in any sense, not simply in connexion with money or the truth, and also to mean decorous, becoming, or appropriate.

Kinde As a noun, this is used by Chaucer to mean 'Nature' (see also under *Nature* below), and the adjective is not to be restricted to its modern associations of tenderness and generosity. Where the noun is used of human beings it is widened in scope to include such meanings as station and group. Lower down in the order of things, with reference to animals, it can mean 'instinct', and implies the divinely sanctioned standards of conduct appropriate to a creature. *Lawe of Kinde* means Natural Law, and in *The Parson's Tale* we find unnatural practices termed 'unkindely'. The Franklin asserts that 'Wommen, of kinde, desiren libertee'—women, by the mere fact of being women, by their sex, desire liberty—and it may be added finally that the word may apply to the sexual organs themselves.

Lered See *Clerk*.

Lewed See *Clerk*.

Nature This abstraction is commonly personified, and it follows the meanings of *Kinde* very closely, since it shares the sense of divine purpose in all its usage. It has the further connotation of 'essential quality' or 'dominating impulse' which leads any creature to continue its way of life. One further implication which may affect the sense of the word is the idea that human impulse may spring from the baser elements in human nature, from which divine grace could free us. Human nature alone received this punishment of sin, and in the sense of 'fallen' nature, as opposed to grace, the word gains a religious significance seemingly at variance with the simpler meaning of impulse and vitality.

Pitee Besides *curteysye*, some other terms that Chaucer uses are affected by *amour courtois*, though most of these are less complex than *curteysye* itself. Here we may mention *Pitee*—not simply pity, but the kindness the all-powerful mistress may come to feel towards her devoted lover, a kindness which may eventually give him some hope of achieving his desires. And secondly *Daunger*: originally, and still sometimes in Chaucer, power such as the lady has over her lover, but also more or less the opposite of *Pitee*: the 'standoffishness' which may prevent her from succumbing to his attentions.[1]

Vertu This word has as its primary meaning a power of strength resident in any person or object, its special nature, quality, or effectiveness. The especial strength of man being his attribute of a soul, it became a word

---

[1] For further information about *amour courtois* terms, see C. S. Lewis, *The Allegory of Love* (Oxford, 1936), ch. 3.

for the particular excellence of the Christian life, and a series of 'virtues' were opposed to 'vices' in the Church's vocabulary.

Vileynye This is used to describe all that is the opposite of *gentil*, *curteys* and *free*. It is the kind of behaviour that one would expect of a completely uncultivated person of the lowest social class, a *cherl* (another common word in this context) or peasant, one who had had no contact with aristocratic ideals of life. Thus it might range from mere external ill-manners or boorishness, through a more fundamental coarseness or brutality, to actual moral evil and sinfulness of all kinds.

Wit This is used by Chaucer to refer to the human mind in general, and also in various specialized senses to refer to the different powers the mind possesses. Thus it may mean understanding or knowledge (and this reminds us of the etymological link between *Wit* and the Chaucerian verb *witen*, to know). Or it may mean the assumption of knowledge, opinion. It may refer to the reliability and prudence of the mind ('wisdom'—another etymologically connected word), or to its opposite qualities of quickness and ingenuity. This last sense is perhaps the nearest to the most common modern meaning of *Wit*; but it is not particularly common in Chaucer, and thus presents a dangerous trap to the unwary reader.

Worthy Nowadays this word is almost invariably used in a patronizing sense; in Chaucer's time it lacked that flavour, and meant simply noble, of genuine worth.

This short list does not even approach completeness. Further help with difficult words in Chaucer may be found in the following works:

J. Copley, *Shift of Meaning* (Oxford).

W. C. Curry, *Chaucer and the Medieval Sciences* (Allen & Unwin)

William Empson, *The Structure of Complex Words* (Chatto & Windus)

C. S. Lewis, *Studies in Words* and *The Discarded Image* (Cambridge) Glossaries and dictionaries of Middle English often provide little help with real difficulties because they simply list alternative meanings; but illumination may often be gained by a reference to *The Oxford Dictionary* or *The Shorter Oxford Dictionary*. For those to whom it is available, the new *Middle English Dictionary*, edited by H. Kurath, S. M. Kuhn, and J. Reidy (Michigan University Press), is invaluable.

BOOKS FOR FURTHER READING

CHAUCER'S ENGLAND (ch. 2)

J. J. Bagley, *Life in Medieval England* (Batsford).
D. S. Brewer, *Chaucer in his Time* (Nelson).
Maurice Hussey, *Chaucer's World, A Pictorial Companion* (Cambridge).
May McKisack, *The Fourteenth Century* (Oxford).
G. Mathew, *The Court of Richard II* (John Murray).
A. R. Myers, *England in the Late Middle Ages* (Penguin Books).
E. Power, *Medieval People* (Penguin Books).
G. M. Trevelyan, *England in the Age of Wycliffe* (Longmans).

THE CHURCH (ch. 3)

David Knowles, *The Religious Orders in England* (Cambridge).
W. A. Pantin, *The English Church in the Fourteenth Century* (Cambridge).

CHAUCER'S LANGUAGE (ch. 4)

A. C. Baugh, *A History of the English Language* (Routledge & Kegan Paul).
O. Jespersen, *The Growth and Structure of the English Language* (Blackwell).
H. Kökeritz, *A Guide to Chaucer's Pronunciation* (Yale University Press).
K. Sisam, *Fourteenth Century Verse and Prose* (Oxford).
J. Wright and E. M. Wright, *An Elementary Middle English Grammar* (Oxford).

CHAUCER'S RHETORIC

J. W. H. Atkins, *English Literary Criticism: the Medieval Phase* (Methuen).
E. R. Curtius, *European Literature and the Latin Middle Ages*, chs. 4, 5 and 8 (Routledge & Kegan Paul).
D. Everett, *Essays on Middle English Literature*, ch. 7 (Oxford).
J. M. Manly, 'Chaucer and the Rhetoricians', *Proceedings of the British Academy*, 1926.
A. C. Spearing, *Criticism and Medieval Poetry*, ch. 3 (Edward Arnold).

CHAUCER THE WRITER (ch. 5)

D. S. Brewer (ed.), *Chaucer and Chaucerians* (Nelson).
W. Clemen, *Chaucer's Early Poetry* (Methuen).
N. Coghill, *The Poet Chaucer* (Oxford).
E. T. Donaldson, *Speaking of Chaucer* (Athlone Press).

W. W. Lawrence, *Chaucer and the Canterbury Tales* (Columbia University Press).

C. S. Lewis, *The Allegory of Love* (Oxford).

J. L. Lowes, *Geoffrey Chaucer* (Oxford).

C. Muscatine, *Chaucer and the French Tradition* (University of California Press).

J. Speirs, *Chaucer the Maker* (Faber & Faber).

CHAUCER'S SCIENCE (ch. 6)

A. C. Crombie, *Augustine to Galileo* (Heinemann).

W. C. Curry, *Chaucer and the Mediaeval Sciences* (Allen & Unwin).

L. Thorndike, *History of Magic and Experimental Science* (Oxford).